CONTENTS

THE FILM

THE CHARACTERS

VEHICLES AND WEAPONS

LOCATIONS

DISNEY PUBLISHING WORLDWIDE GLOBAL MAGAZINES, COMICS AND PARTWORKS
Publisher Lynn Waggoner
Editorial Director Bianca Coletti
Director, Comics Guido Frazzini
Executive Editor, New IP Stefano Ambrosio
Executive Editor, Franchise Carlotta Quattrocolo
Senior Manager, Editorial Development Camilla Vedove
Senior Editor Behnoosh Khalili
Senior Editor Julie Dorris
Senior Designer Enrico Soave
VP, Global Art Ken Shue
Creative Director Roberto Santillo
Creative Manager Marco Ghiglione
Creative Manager Manny Mederos
Computer Art Designer Stefano Attardi
Director Olivia Ciancarelli
Senior Manager, Franchise Mariantonietta Galla
Editorial Manager Virpi Korhonen
Text Alessandro Ferrari
Graphic Design n co-d S.r.l. – Milano
Pre=Press co-d S.r.l. – Milano, Lito milano srl

LUCASFILM
Senior Editor Brett Rector
Image Archives Newell Todd, Tim Mapp, Nicole LaCoursiere
Story Group Pablo Hidalgo, Leland Chee, Matt Martin
Special Thanks: Lynne Hale, Connie Wethington, Natalie Kocekian, Brian Miller, Michael Siglain, Heather West, Gabrielle Levenson

TITAN EDITORIAL
Editor Jonathan Wilkins
Senior Executive Editor Divinia Fleary
Art Editor Andrew Leung
Copy Editor Simon Hugo
Editorial Assistant Tolly Maggs
Senior Production Controller Jackie Flook
Production Supervisor Maria Pearson
Production Controller Peter James
Art Director Oz Browne
Subscription Executive Tony Ho
Senior Sales Manager Steve Tothill
Direct Sales & Marketing Manager Ricky Claydon
Brand Manager Marketing Lucy Ripper
Commercial Manager Michelle Fairlamb
Advertising Assistant Tom Miller
U.S. Advertising Manager Jeni Smith
Publishing Manager Darryl Tothill
Publishing Director Chris Teather
Operations Director Leigh Baulch
Executive Director Vivian Cheung
Publisher Nick Landau

DISTRIBUTION
US Newsstand: Total Publisher Services, Inc. John Dziewiatkowski, 630-851-7683
US Distribution: Ingram Periodicals, Curtis Circulation Company
UK Newsstand: Comag, 01895 444 055
US/UK Direct Sales Market: Diamond Comic Distributors
For more info on advertising contact adinfo@titanemail.com

For sale in the US, Canada, UK and Eire

Star Wars: A New Hope The Official Celebration Special Published September 2017 by Titan Magazines, a division of Titan Publishing Group Limited, 144 Southwark Street, London SE1 0UP

ISBN: 9781785864605

Printed in China

A CIP catalogue record for this title is available from the British Library

10 9 8 7 6 5 4 3 2

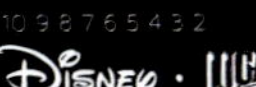

STAR WARS THE MYTH

On May 25, 1977, the day *Star Wars* (later titled Episode IV *A New Hope)* was released, everything changed for audiences all over the world.

There simply was no other film in the 1970s like *Star Wars.* There were fantasy movies of course; war movies and westerns; big spiritual stories with ties to mythological archetypes; and sci-fi films with elaborate sets and costumes, with alien creatures, dinosaurs, or highly evolved apes—even animatronic robots.

But *Star Wars* was the first to put all of these elements together, creating a new, original universe—an epic dimension able to appeal to adults and kids alike. Moreover, state-of-the-art special effects of a kind that had previously been considered too expensive and unprofitable by movie studios came into their own, playing a crucial role in a blockbuster motion picture for the first time.

The success of George Lucas' vision changed the film industry forever, encouraging investment in merchandising and special effects, and the development of new technologies such as CGI (computer-generated imagery). It also established a whole new mythology that is still inspiring new generations of filmmakers, writers, and artists to this day. With *A New Hope*, a new era of entertainment had dawned.

1 /

2 /

1 / *Star Wars* teaser poster, December 1976. Twentieth Century-Fox had planned to open the film around the Fourth of July weekend—when kids were out of school. But Lucas wanted his film to be released in May, for Memorial Day weekend, so that kids would see the film and then talk about it at school.

2 / One of the *Star Wars* paintings by artist Tommy Jung that was used for posters and other publicity material.

STAR WARS BY THE NUMBERS

365 Total special effects shots

117 Minutes for the first cut

950 Paid employees

84 Total days of shooting

42 Hours of performance by the London Symphony Orchestra and John Williams to record the soundtrack

32 Theaters where *Star Wars* opened on May 25, 1977

12 Minutes of screen time featuring Darth Vader

2187 Leia's cell number, named for Arthur Lipsett's short movie *21-87*, which deeply influenced George Lucas

$750 Harrison Ford's weekly salary

$850 Carrie Fisher's weekly salary

$1,000 Mark Hamill's weekly salary

$50,000 Lucas' salary as writer

$72,700 Lucas' salary as director

$93,000 Stormtroopers budget

$220,000 Wardrobe budget

$3,619,601 Industrial Light & Magic budget

$8,228,228 Projected budget

$11,293,151 Final budget

$254,809 Opening day box office

$2,500,000 Six-day box office

$786,598,007 Worldwide box office

STRUCTURING *STAR WARS*

When writing the script for *Star Wars*, Lucas used a simple three-act structure, inspired by the classic "Hero's Journey" narrative. A favorite of storytellers since ancient times, the Hero's Journey can be found in countless myths and fables. It sees a protagonist with an ordinary life step into the unknown to face trials and challenges that transform him into a powerful hero.

ACT ONE

In which the setting is created. The hero and his everyday world, the main characters, and their relationship are introduced, along with the conflict that moves the story forward.

> "A long time ago, in a galaxy far far away...."

An Imperial Star Destroyer captures Princess Leia's ship. Before the Emperor's emissary, Darth Vader, finds the princess, she loads the stolen plans of an Imperial superweapon—a space station called the Death Star—into the droid R2-D2. He and another droid, C-3PO, flee in an escape pod and land on the planet Tatooine, where they are bought by a farmer and his nephew, Luke Skywalker. Luke inadvertently activates a message in R2-D2, in which Leia asks for help from Obi-Wan Kenobi. The little droid goes off in search of Kenobi, and Luke and C-3PO follow. They are attacked by Tusken Raiders, but an old man arrives and scares the desert dwellers away. He reveals himself to be Obi-Wan, one of the Jedi Knights who were once the guardians of peace in the galaxy. He says that Luke's late father was also a Jedi, who was killed when Darth Vader, Obi-Wan's former apprentice, turned to evil. Obi-Wan gives Luke his father's lightsaber and says that he must learn the ways of the Force, an energy field that can give a Jedi special powers. Luke is reluctant, and refuses to join Obi-Wan in answering Leia's plea, which asks him to deliver the plans for the Death Star to the Rebel Alliance on the planet Alderaan. However, Luke changes his mind when he learns that Imperial stormtroopers sent to track down the two droids have killed his uncle and aunt.

The major event that ends the first act marks the beginning of the formerly reluctant protagonist's journey in a new world.

ACT TWO

In which the hero tries to solve the problem at the heart of his quest, but fails because he does not yet have the abilities needed to defeat the antagonist. The situation worsens.

Together with the droids, Luke and Obi-Wan reach the spaceport of Mos Eisley where, in a crowded cantina, they hire Han Solo and his co-pilot Chewbacca to take them to Alderaan. Han, the owner of a ship called the *Millennium Falcon*, needs the job to pay off a debt that could cost him his life. En route, Obi-Wan teaches Luke to trust the Force more than his senses. Before they can reach their destination, however, Imperial Governor Tarkin uses the Death Star to destroy Alderaan. When they arrive, Luke and the others find only debris—and the vast Death Star itself, which easily captures the *Falcon* in a tractor beam. When the ship is brought onto the space station, our heroes sneak out. Obi-Wan locates and disables the source of the tractor beam, while Luke, Han and

ACT ONE

ACT ONE

ACT TWO

ACT THREE

Chewbacca find and rescue Leia, who is being held prisoner on board. To give the others time to escape, Obi-Wan engages in lightsaber combat with Darth Vader, then lets Vader take his life. The *Falcon* flees the Death Star, but a tracking beacon has been hidden aboard.

The second act in the classic Hero's Journey ends in tragedy. All hope seems lost.

ACT THREE

In which the hero—with the help of his companions and some supernatural intervention—is reborn with new confidence and ability. He faces the antagonist once again and this time he is victorious. In the end, his world has completely changed.

Leia leads Luke and his friends to the rebel base on Yavin 4, but the Death Star is not far behind. Analyzing the stolen plans, the rebels discover the space station's weakness. Luke and a squadron of rebel pilots attack the Death Star while Han leaves to pay his debt. Darth Vader attacks Luke's ship just as he is about to strike the Death Star's weak point. But Han and Chewbacca join the fight in time to save him. Luke hears Obi-Wan's voice urging him to use the Force. He closes his eyes, fires, and destroys the Death Star. Later, Leia awards Luke and Han with medals for their heroism.

BEFORE STAR WARS

Born in 1944 and raised in the rural town of Modesto, California, George Lucas has always been fascinated by outer-space adventures. He graduated from the University of Southern California's School of Cinema in 1967, then started an internship at Warner Bros., where he befriended the older film-school graduate Francis Ford Coppola. In 1968, while working as production assistant for Coppola's *The Rain People*, Lucas was also working on his first feature as writer and director, *THX 1138*. It was while working on this dystopian sci-fi movie set in the 25th century that he first spoke about a new idea for a film featuring holograms and spaceships.

At some point after he finished his second feature film, *American Graffiti* (1973), George Lucas realized that very few films were being made for young people and, of the ones that were being made, none were anything like the movies he had grown up with in the 1950s—Westerns, outer-space fantasies, and pirate movies.

Together with comic books and pulp fiction, such movies had had a lasting effect on the young Lucas, with powerful imagery that made him feel good and inspired him to dream. So, instead of continuing with the movie about the Vietnam War he had planned to make next (*Apocalypse Now*, which Francis Ford Coppola would later direct) Lucas started to write a new, more optimistic story. He envisioned it as an update of the mythic tales that had informed his childhood favorites, believing that a new generation of younger moviegoers would respond to the same things that had so moved him. And so, *Star Wars* was born.

Starting with the concept of a tyrannical empire going after a small group of freedom fighters, Lucas set about writing a two-page concept called *Journal of the Whills, [Part] I.* This was "the story of Mace Windy, a revered Jedi-Bendu of Ophuchi, as related to us by C. J. Thorpe, padawaan learner to the famed Jedi."

Many now-familiar elements were already present in these two brief pages: the Jedi, the Galactic Empire and the concept of "will" (as in "willing things to happen") which would become the Force. In May 1973, Lucas finished the first full treatment of these ideas, introducing a space fortress, civil wars, an experienced Jedi general, a rebel princess, and a weapon he called a "lazer sword."

The rough draft of *"The Star Wars"* (as originally written) was completed a year later, in May 1974, followed by the first draft in July. From its beginnings as an escape movie (in which a general and a princess on the run from the Galactic Empire travel to a neutral planet), it became a rescue movie in which Princess Leia, captured halfway through the film, has to be rescued from Alderaan, the capital of the Empire. Characters such as the young hero Annikin Starkiller, Darth Vader, the Knights of the Sith, and "Grande Mouff" Tarkin appear—together with an updated concept of "will" called "the force of others." The words "May the force of others be with you" are spoken in dialogue.

A breakthrough came in 1975, with the second draft: "*Adventures of the Starkiller, Episode I: The Star Wars.*" Here, "the force of others" takes on a more familiar ▸

1 / A production painting by illustrator Ralph McQuarrie, who was hired to visualize Lucas' story and help producer Gary Kurtz formulate a budget. Based on the revisions of the second draft script, the illustration depicts the five main characters at that time: Corellian pirate Han Solo holding a lightsaber, his co-pilot Chewbacca, the droids C-3PO and R2-D2, and Luke Starkiller as a young girl. (See previous page.)

2 / George Lucas (left of center) in front of a full-size X-wing starfighter at Shepperton Studios in Surrey, England. From 1973, Lucas planned to shoot an epic battle between spaceships and sought out footage of World War II dogfights and other flights, which he edited into a 16mm reference film that fit his own story. Before *Star Wars*, most space battle scenes were unrealistically static.

3 / Lucas poses with the prototype for droid R2-D2 in 1975. Lucas' early films were avant-garde documentaries and abstract shorts with a pessimistic outlook, but the response to his nostalgic teen drama *American Graffiti* made him realize how much kids needed a positive story packed full of humor and heroes.

4 / George Lucas on the Death Star elevator set. The title "*The Star Wars*" was registered with the Motion Picture Association of America (MPAA) on August 3, 1971, by United Artists—the first studio with which Lucas signed an agreement for the film.

5 / Director George Lucas and actor Mark Hamill confer on the Tatooine set in the Tunisian desert. (See opposite page.)

2 /

3 /

4 /

form, described as a "powerful energy field" believed to influence all living creatures. It manifested in two forms: "Ashla," which was good, and harnessed by the Jedi, and "Bogan," which was evil and used by the bad guys. A significant development, "Bogan" made the villains as powerful as the hero, thereby making the journey and the victory much more satisfying.

At the same time, Lucas also reined in the scope of the story—starting the second draft at a point that hadn't occurred until halfway through before. His new beginning was a scene where two robots flee from a rebel ship being chased by Imperial Star Destroyers. He also took out the princess, and added the "Kiber Crystal," a diamond-like source of life and powers. Now, "Luke Starkiller" had to take this crystal to his father, a mighty Jedi warrior known simply as "The Starkiller."

The second draft was modified consistently between March and May 1975. With no princess, the Luke character became a girl, but then changed back into Luke as the princess was reintroduced. The third draft, "*The Star Wars: From the Adventures of Luke Starkiller*," is dated August 1975. By then, production had already begun and Lucas was hiring cameramen and art directors, and building his own special-effects house. The revised story focused on Luke's journey of self-discovery, from learning about the Force to destroying the Death Star. This new emphasis reduced the role of the Kiber Crystal, which vanished for the fourth draft, *The Adventures of Luke Starkiller as Taken from the "Journal of the Whills" (Saga I)*.

Written during 1975 and 1976, while Lucas was busy interviewing actors, and supervising the building of sets, the creation of aliens, and the special effects unit, this fourth draft defined the Force as a field surrounding every creature, which could be joined upon death. To learn how the Force works, Luke would have to trust his feelings rather than his logic. The draft also came with a fairytale intro to drive home the mythic nature of the story: "A long, long time ago in a galaxy far, far away," it read, "an incredible adventure took place." Finally, the pieces were in place to create a legend.

6 /

7 /

6 / Sir Alec Guinness and George Lucas on set, on March 26, 1976, waiting to film Ben Kenobi's first scene – his arrival in the Tatooine canyon.

7 / Hamill, Lucas, and Ford on Stage 2 of Elstree Studios, in front of the Death Star elevator.

8 / Lucas instructing Peter Mayhew, Mark Hamill, and Harrison Ford on the Death Star detention-block set.

9 / Guinness, Hamill, and Lucas on the set of Ben Kenobi's house, which was supposed to be a bizarre three-story cave carved out of rock before the budget cuts.

8 /

9 /

C-3PO

There may be countless protocol droids in the galaxy—all programmed to aid their masters by translating alien and cyborg languages and providing valuable information about costumes and etiquette—but C-3PO is a droid unlike any other. While his only desire is to stay out of trouble and not get caught up in any kind of adventure, his destiny is to become one of the central figures in the events that lead to the Rebellion's most important victory against the Galactic Empire. Fluent in six million forms of communication, including the ones used by computer systems on spaceships like the *Millennium Falcon*, C-3PO is valued as a linguist, but most of all as a loyal ally. His devotion to his masters and friendship with R2-D2 are his greatest assets. Together, the droids make a capable team that the Empire underestimates at its cost.

The name C-3PO, or "Seethreepio" as originally written, together with "Artwo Deetwo," first appears in George Lucas' notes in 1974, while he was working on the rough draft of the story that would become *Star Wars*. At first, both characters were envisioned as workmen, but then Lucas reimagined them as two very different robots.

Inspired by his love of classic cinema, Lucas pictured C-3PO with a look similar to Maria, the mechanical woman in Fritz Lang's silent expressionist masterpiece, *Metropolis* (1927). Following Lucas' descriptions of C-3PO as a more "human robot" alongside the "robot robot" look of R2-D2, concept designer and illustrator Ralph McQuarrie drew his first sketches of the characters in 1974. In January the following year, he finished the first key illustration for the film, featuring R2-D2 and C-3PO walking away from their escape pod in the Tatooine desert.

McQuarrie's paintings and sketches provided the basis for the work of special mechanical effects supervisor John Stears, production designer John Barry, and sculptor Liz Moore, who finalized C-3PO's design in 1976. Lucas approved the design when he hit upon the comical expression he was after by adding two coins as the eyes.

The art department modeled the C-3PO costume on the body of the actor who would play the part—Anthony Daniels. A British actor at the National Theatre of Great Britain, Daniels had first met Lucas in 1975. Among the skills that won him the role were his mastery of mime—a valuable asset for a droid with only one facial expression. Daniels read the script and was immediately excited about the character, realizing that C-3PO was something that had never been seen in a movie before.

When filming began, Lucas realized that C-3PO needed to move whenever he spoke, so it was obvious where his voice was coming from. This was hard for Daniels, as the metal outfit made even the most simple movements very difficult. The costume was so thick and uncomfortable that, if C-3PO wasn't fully in a shot, the actor would wear only the necessary part of it, be it an arm, or the head and shoulders.

There was no way to redesign the costume once on set, and so it continued to cause problems throughout the shoot. A simple scene where C-3PO had to pick up a comlink to talk to Luke on the Death Star (scene 94, shot in June 1976) called for 20 takes, and, eventually, a hidden sticky pad in the droid's metal hand, in order to get the blink-and-you-miss-it shot. Luckily for Daniels, he was wearing only the one hand for the duration!

C-3PO DATA FILE

DAYS OF SHOOTING: 54

COSTUME BUDGET: $18,189 (£7,750)

FIRST LINE: "Did you hear that? They've shut down the main reactor. We'll be destroyed for sure. This is madness!" (Spoken to R2-D2 aboard the *Tantive IV*, as it is attacked by Imperial forces.)

LAST LINE: "You must repair him! Sir, if any of my circuits or gears will help, I'll gladly donate them." (Referring to the badly damaged R2-D2, as the droid returns from the successful attack on the Death Star.)

TRIVIA: Anthony Daniels plays C-3PO in every *Star Wars* film, including *Rogue One: A Star Wars Story*.

2 /

3 /

1 / On the first day of shooting, it took two hours for Daniels to put on the costume. Once inside, he could not sit down, so when he was not acting the crew put him on a leaning board. As filming went on, the time Daniels needed to dress for a shot came down to half an hour. (See previous page.)

2 / C-3PO's head was attached to both the chest and back pieces. The left arm hole was built into the chest piece, and the right arm hole was part of the back panel.

3 / R2-D2 and C-3PO walk away from their escape pod into the desert of Tatooine, in artist Ralph McQuarrie's first key illustration for *Star Wars*. McQuarrie brought George Lucas' character descriptions to life using a mix of gouache, watercolors, and acrylics, and added many design elements and details of his own.

4 / By the end of the first day of filming in March 1976, C-3PO actor Anthony Daniels was covered in scars and scratches from the droid costume. It was the one and only time that he wore the outfit for a whole day.

5/ Scene 15, in which C-3PO crosses the desert and walks past the bleached bones of a huge creature, was shot on the second day. Anthony Daniels could barely move, and as soon as he went off camera, behind a sand dune, he fell over.

4 /

5 /

R2-D2

Astromech units are multipurpose droids found throughout the galaxy. Programmed to repair computers, retrieve information, and assist starfighter pilots as navigators, they communicate only through electronic beeps and whistles that are usually translated by protocol droids. Built by Industrial Automaton, R2-D2 looks just like any other astromech droid, but has exceeded his programming to develop a daring, stubborn, and sometimes sarcastic personality. Loved and trusted by the likes of Leia and Luke, R2-D2 is loyal and motivated, and always willing to risk his circuits to complete a mission or help his masters—especially when it involves defeating Imperial forces. Unlike some other droids, R2-D2 is also good at keeping secrets, even from his near-constant counterpart, C-3PO.

While working on the second draft of the story that would become *Star Wars* (completed in January 1975), George Lucas realized that the two droids that flee a small rebel ship when it comes under attack had to become more than just the comic relief. In fact, the story itself had to be told from their point of view. And so, R2-D2 and C-3PO—the former in particular—became the through-line of the picture, going on the same journey of discovery as the audience, meeting one main character after another.

Just like his protocol droid companion, R2-D2's design was based on concept art by Ralph McQuarrie, who created detailed paintings based on George Lucas' descriptions. McQuarrie depicted the droid as a compact "garbage can" with three short legs, and in August 1975 production designer John Barry set about building the non-humanoid robot for real at Pinewood Studios in England.

Along with special mechanical effects supervisor John Stears, Barry built a cardboard mock-up of the droid, before liaising with British actor Kenny Baker for an actual working prototype. As the man who would be inside the finished unit, the 3 ft 5in Baker gave Barry and Stears a vital insight about what was feasible for an actor in such a small space. As a result of their collaboration, Barry and Stears went on to build a second mechanical unit.

On set, the mechanical unit was controlled remotely for the scenes in which R2-D2 had to roll along on three legs, with Baker directly controlling the droid whenever it needed to turn its head, walk, or light up. The lights were designed to convey different emotional reactions (excitement, fear, and curiosity), so that the character would come across as "more than just a robot."

These same emotions later helped sound designer Ben Burtt create R2-D2's distinctive voice. After many unsuccessful attempts, Burtt finally hit upon the perfect sound by blending inarticulate human vocalizations with notes played on a state-of-the-art synthesizer keyboard.

1 / Kenny Baker inside R2-D2 during a break from filming the Yavin 4 throne room scene. (See previous page.)

2 / Kenny Baker inside R2-D2 on the first day of shooting in Tunisia. Baker wore a harness that secured the R2-D2 unit to his body, and custom-made boots that linked his legs to the droid's feet so that they moved as one.

3 / R2-D2 wasn't the only mechanical droid on set in Tunisia. The R5-D4 unit had similarly complex innards, which made it unsuitable for use in the scene where it was scripted to blow up. Instead, a fiberglass backup unit was fitted with an exploding stunt head and pulled along on piano wire.

4 / The mechanical R2-D2 was carefully designed, but never really worked during filming. On the very first day in Tunisia, its batteries ran out too soon, and its third leg didn't work at all. Also, throughout the shoot, all of the mechanical units kept picking up interference, such as radio stations, and so couldn't be remote-controlled until they were reworked. (See opposite page.)

2 /

R2-D2 DATA FILE

FIRST DAY OF SHOOTING:
March 22, 1976

LAST DAY OF SHOOTING:
July 17, 1976

George Lucas wanted R2-D2 to sound like a five-year-old kid.

R2-D2's name comes from "Reel 2, Dialogue 2," a filmreel George Lucas was looking for one night while working late on his directorial debut, THX 1138.

Kenny Baker's friend and longtime cabaret partner Jack Purvis played the chief Jawa.

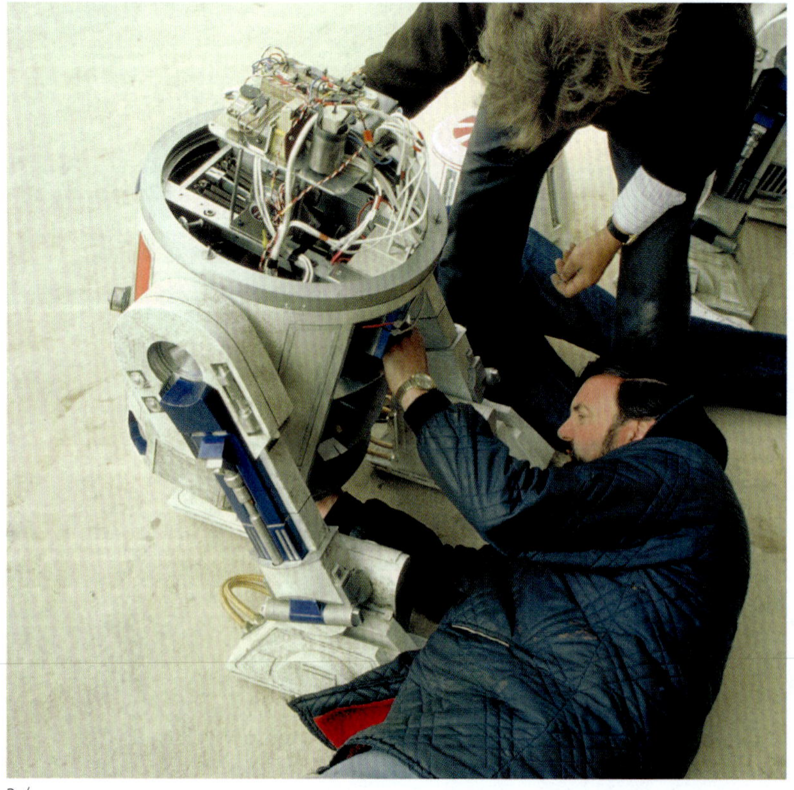

3 /

DARTH VADER
BEHIND THE MASK

Though the Jedi and the Sith are considered extinct—with the Force nothing more than an ancient religion—Darth Vader continues to instill fear and reverence into the Imperial troops and officers that serve under him. A long time ago, Vader turned to the dark side, and his body was badly damaged in a duel with his former Jedi Master, Obi-Wan Kenobi. Now he survives as a cyborg, his limbs and vital organs dependent on a life-support suit and a terrifying helmet fitted with a speech projector and mechanical breathing apparatus. He is far from weak, however, commanding a fearsome knowledge of the Force that allows him to control the weak-minded, move objects with his thoughts, and even choke his opponents from afar. This, along with his prowess with a lightsaber, makes him the Emperor's most powerful emissary.

George Lucas put an Imperial general at the heart of his story for *Star Wars* right from the start. In 1973, this general was called Owen Lars, a name Lucas would later use for Luke's uncle. The general became Darth Vader in 1974 and finally "Lord Darth Vader, right hand to the Master of the Sith" in January 1975.

Yet it was only in January 1976, with the fourth and final draft, that the character was fully realized, becoming a man-machine. Lucas had figured out his backstory by then: Vader had killed Luke's father, before being confronted by Ben Kenobi and falling into a volcanic pit. This explained Vader's suit and mask—as depicted in one of concept artist Ralph McQuarrie's key illustrations—but also let Lucas address a theme that had always interested him: Man's relationship to machines. "A machine is only as bad as the man that sits behind it," he said. "It's an extension of mankind, and if it develops bad technology, it's because the mind behind it was bad." And so, the Lord of the Sith was born.

McQuarrie painted the key illustration that created Darth Vader's legendary look during February 1975. Lucas described the character to him as a "dark fluttering figure," adding that both Vader and his opponent needed to wear masks, as they would battle from ship to ship, jumping through the vacuum of space. Following this direction, McQuarrie conceived the dark space suit that became a defining part of the character. ▸

2 /

3 /

DARTH VADER DATA FILE

COSTUME BUDGET: $1,173 (£500)

FIRST LINE: "Where are those transmissions you intercepted? What have you done with those plans?" (As he lifts an unlucky rebel by the throat.)

LAST LINE: "What?!" (In surprise, as the Millennium Falcon unexpectedly stops him from shooting down Luke.)

Vader was not Lucas' first cyborg character. In his second draft, Ben Kenobi was a half-man, half-machine general.

A scene cut from the fourth draft showed Darth Vader in a crystal chamber talking to the Sith Knights, who hunted down Jedi Knights across the galaxy.

The final design for Vader's suit and mask was closely based on the design created by McQuarrie, but with refinements by costume designer John Mollo. Mollo had extensive experience of military uniforms and he and his team scoured theatrical costumers to find and photograph army surplus and other items that could work for the characters before showing them to Lucas for approval. For Darth Vader, they located a black motorcycle suit, a Nazi helmet, a gas mask, and a monk's cloak. Using these reference points, the costumers then made the basic leather costume, while Mollo made the mask, the armor, the belt, and the chest plate.

A British bodybuilder, David Prowse, was cast to play the role of Vader, having originally been approached to play Chewbacca. Ironically, Prowse turned down the Wookiee role because it was a masked character, not realizing that neither his face nor voice would feature as Vader, either. He began shooting in April 1976, at Elstree Studios in England. His first scene was also the first to be filmed on the Death Star set, with Vader pursuing Obi-Wan Kenobi inside the battle station.

The actor chosen to provide Darth Vader's voice was James Earl Jones, whose commanding, deep voice was exactly what Lucas was looking for. Jones found the right tone by reducing Vader's expressive range as a reflection of his lack of humanity. All of Jones' dialogue was recorded in about two and a half hours on March 1, 1977, at Goldwyn Studios in West Hollywood.

Once recorded, Vader's voice was put through a process called "worldizing" created by sound designer Walter Murch for Lucas' previous film, *American Graffiti*. This involved re-recording the voice track as it played out in an everyday room to give it a more realistic sound. Sound designer Ben Burtt then used tubes and aqualungs to create the labored breathing that would become the character's trademark.

4 /

5 /

1 / The Dark Lord of the Sith went through various name changes before George Lucas settled on Darth Vader. One early possibility was "Dark Water." Lucas then started to use Darth as a prefix, adding different last names before hitting on the combination of "Darth" and "Vader." (See page 23.)

2 / Concept art by Ralph McQuarrie not only helped to define Vader's look but also visualised the idea of a "lazer-sword" duel. When this image was painted, McQuarrie was using the second draft as a reference, and that described such a duel between Darth Vader and Deak Starkiller. Deak was the brother of Annikin Starkiller, who would later change his name to Luke Skywalker. In the same way, Vader's opponent would later become Obi-Wan "Ben" Kenobi. (See previous spread.)

3 / Dave Prowse and Alec Guinness duel as Darth Vader and Obi-Wan Kenobi on the Death Star set. (See opposite page.)

4 / Darth Vader at the controls of his TIE Advanced starfighter.

5 / Dave Prowse in costume alongside Leslie Schofield as General Bast.

LUKE SKYWALKER

A "farm boy" who craves adventure and excitement, Luke Skywalker lives on Tatooine, a desert world seemingly far removed from the struggle between the Empire and the Rebel Alliance. Having grown up on a moisture farm with his Uncle Owen and Aunt Beru, Luke thinks that his only hope of getting off the planet is to go to the Imperial Academy and become a pilot like his old friend Biggs Darklighter (who plans to join the rebels when he graduates). But every time he's about to apply, his uncle convinces him to stay on and help with the farm for another season. Owen knows that Luke was not born to be a farmer, but is afraid that the boy will turn out like his father, who was an ill-fated Jedi Knight—and not the navigator on a freighter, as Luke believes. A chance meeting with two droids leads Luke to a Jedi who knew his father, and his life changes forever.

In 1974, George Lucas' rough draft for the story of *Star Wars* named Luke Skywalker as a 60-year-old Jedi general, and Annikin Starkiller as an 18-year-old boy soon to become his "padawan" apprentice. Annikin was not the main character in the story, but was part of a cast that included his brother, Deak, and his father, the dying Jedi Kane Starkiller, who had mechanical body parts like Darth Vader.

By the time Lucas started to write the second draft, he had already changed Annikin's name to Luke and made him into the protagonist. "Luke reluctantly accepts the burden (artist, not a warrior, fear)," he wrote in his early notes. "Establish Luke as a good pilot... farm boy: fulfills the legend of the son of the sons; pulls the sword from the stone. All he wants in life is to become a starpilot." He also introduced Luke's twin brothers, Biggs and Windy, at this point, along with his 16-year-old cousin, Leia.

In the third draft, 1975's *The Star Wars: From the Adventures of Luke Starkiller*, Annikin is the name of Luke's dead father and Luke—who didn't know Annikin was a Jedi—is now an only son. Changing Luke's family makeup in this way not only defined the character as a loner, but also drew attention to his origins—which were intrinsically linked to his future path as a Jedi.

For his fourth draft, Lucas refined Luke's journey further, taking his lead from the book he was reading: Joseph Campbell's academic study of story structure, *The Hero with a Thousand Faces.* In the book, Campbell details an archtypal hero's journey common to many mythic tales. Key beats in Campbell's structure include: 'Call to Adventure' (for example, Luke hearing Leia ask for help), 'Refusal of the Call' (Luke saying he can't go to Alderaan), 'Belly of the Whale' (Luke and friends are drawn into the Death Star), and 'The Road of Trials' (Luke faces various perils on the Death Star). Each step of this journey changes the protagonist in some way, shaping him into a hero.

Throughout all these changes, Luke had retained the last name "Starkiller." In April 1975, with many scenes already shot, Lucas changed this to "Skywalker," on the grounds that "Starkiller" was far too antagonistic for a Jedi. ▸

2 /

3 /

1 / Mark Hamill as Luke Skywalker on the *Millennium Falcon* set. (See previous spread.)

2 / Mark Hamill with Anthony Daniels inside the C-3PO costume in Tunisia. On day five of the shoot, Hamill realized his character was very like George Lucas and started to draw inspiration from him. Lucas then began to call Hamill "The Kid" —a name people had called him before he grew a beard.

3 / Just like his father, Luke was always an ace pilot. Before he joined the rebels' Red Squadron, he raced through the canyons of Tatooine in a tri-wing T-16 skyhopper.

4 / Harrison Ford and Mark Hamill on set for the trash compactor scene. The dianoga creature that grabs Luke was originally scripted as a semi-transparent beast in a watery cave on the planet Alderaan. But budgetary constraints led to the cave and trash room scenes being combined, and just one tentacle of the monster being seen on screen. (See opposite page.)

When casting sessions began in 1975, Lucas didn't have anyone in mind to play Luke Skywalker. He just wanted his hero to look shorter and younger than Han Solo, who was supposed to be in his 20s. During three weeks of auditions, Lucas and casting director Dianne Crittenden saw well-known actors such as John Travolta, Tommy Lee Jones, and Nick Nolte. The director Brian DePalma aided them in their search, which even saw them interviewing people with no prior acting experience.

Twenty-four-year-old Mark Hamill was not among these complete newcomers, as he was already starring in *The Texas Wheelers* on TV, but he was one of the thousands of auditionees to be seen and then dismissed. Long after his initial 15-minute interview, however, Hamill was called back in December 1975, and asked to read four pages of dialogue alongside Harrison Ford as Han Solo. Lucas thought that Ford was right for the part of Solo, but he wasn't going to cast any of his main characters until he had tested them all together.

The rapport between Hamill and Ford perfectly captured the relationship he wanted for Luke and Han, and it was this, along with Hamill's naïve, idealistic attitude, that convinced Lucas to cast him in January 1976—surprising Hamill, who was sure he hadn't gotten the part. ▸

4 /

LUKE SKYWALKER DATA FILE

DAYS OF SHOOTING: 70

FIRST LINE:
"It looks like we don't have much of a choice, but I'll remind him." (In reply to Aunt Beru, who asks Luke to tell his Uncle Owen to buy a droid that can speak the Bocce language.)

LAST LINE:
"He'll be all right." (Reassuring C-3PO when R2-D2 returns damaged after the rebel assault on the Death Star.)

TRIVIA:
"Luke Skywalker" was the last character name in the movie to be finalized.

As originally scripted, the destruction of the Death Star called for Luke to drop a bomb through a hatch on the station's surface, then defeat Darth Vader in a swordfight to escape.

Among the lines Mark Hamill had to learn for his casting test were: "We can't turn back. Fear is their greatest defense. I doubt if the actual security there is any greater than it was on Aquilae or Sullust. What there is, is most likely directed toward a large-scale assault."

6 /

Luke's life on Tatooine had to be carefully constructed to convince audiences that the Tunisian desert was really an alien world. Key to this was Luke's landspeeder—an anti-grav craft that was everyday to him, but thrillingly different for even seasoned moviegoers.

The first landspeeder built by production designer John Barry was big enough for four people, but Lucas wanted something less grand—more suited to a young farm boy, and to moving through the narrow Tunisian streets on location.

With the design finalized, the functioning vehicle was built by a car company in England. It ran on standard car wheels, but these were hidden in long shots using a mirrored skirt that reflected the ground beneath it. For close-ups, special effects supervisor John Stears and art director Les Dilley mounted the vehicle on a carousel, sustaining the illusion that it was hovering all the time.

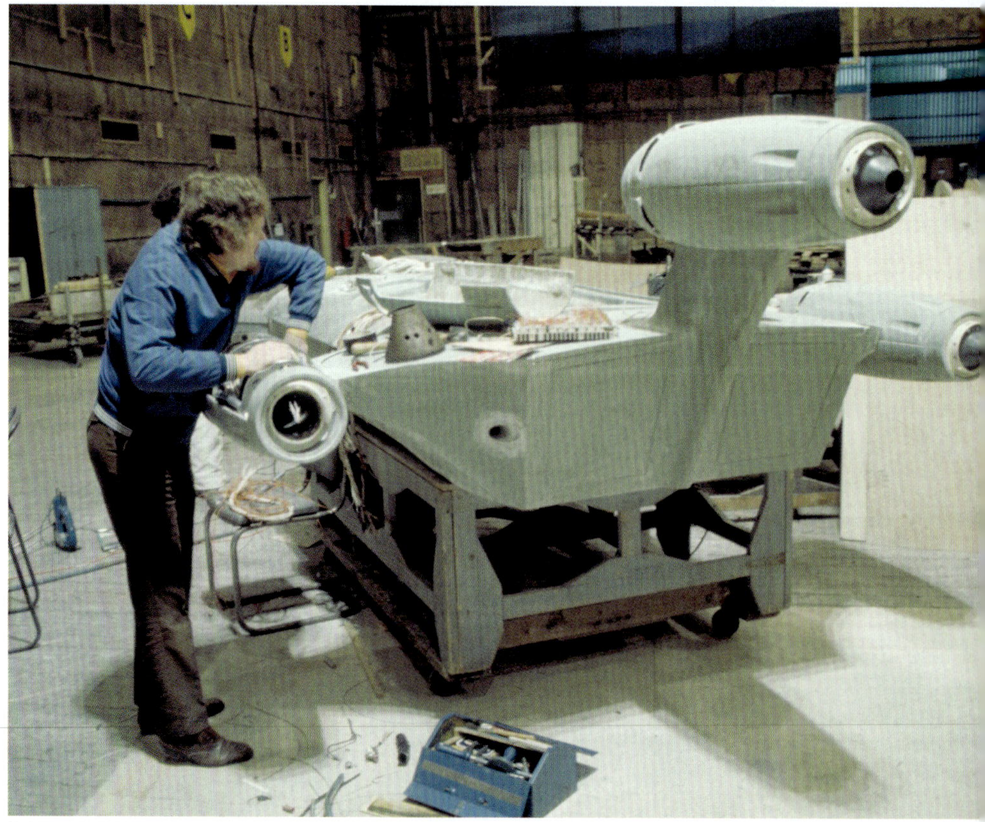

7 /

8 /

5 / Luke Skywalker climbs to the gunner position on board the *Millennium Falcon*. (See previous spread.)

6 / One of the first three-wheeled land-speeder prototypes built by Industrial Light & Magic (ILM). (See opposite page.)

7 / The final, full-size speeder being built to a design originally drawn by production designer John Barry. (See opposite page.)

8 / ILM's Bill Shourt and Richard Alexander prepare to take the finished, functioning landspeeder prop for a spin around the ILM parking lot in Van Nuys, California.

9 / Actors Mark Hamill, Anthony Daniels, and Alec Guinness in the landspeeder during filming in Tunisia.

9 /

OBI-WAN KENOBI

To his distant neighbors on Tatooine, "Ben" Kenobi is just a crazy old wizard, living like a hermit in the dangerous Jundland Wastes. In truth, however, he was a Jedi Knight in the last years of the Galactic Republic. He went by the name of Obi-Wan Kenobi, and was master to Darth Vader before he turned to the dark side. A hero in the Clone Wars, he knew Princess Leia's father Bail Organa, and is one of the few to know the truth about Luke Skywalker and his father. For years, Kenobi has watched over the farm boy, waiting for the day he could teach him about the Force and pass him the lightsaber once owned by Luke's father—an elegant weapon from an earlier time, used only by the Jedi and their enemies, the Sith.

The Jedi general, the princess, and the boy were among the first characters George Lucas created for *Star Wars* in 1973. At first, the Jedi general was the protagonist, taking the princess to a neutral planet and cutting alien enemies in half with his "lazer sword." But, as his ideas developed, Lucas lessened the importance of the character, and then cut him out altogether.

By the third draft, written in 1975, the general was back, now a half-man half-machine called Ben Kenobi. He had a major role as Luke's mentor, taking the boy as a "padawan" and training him in the ways of the Force. The old man remained a central part of the hero's journey in the fourth draft, completed in January 1976, but was no longer a cyborg.

In this new draft, Kenobi had previously been hunted across the galaxy by Darth Vader. He and Luke saved Princess Leia from the Death Star, but while they were escaping, he was wounded in a swordfight with Vader. Only with Luke's help did he make it out alive on the *Millennium Falcon.*

It was only during the second week of shooting in Tunisia in the spring of 1976 that Lucas realized the story needed a major revision. The relatively painless escape from the Death Star diminished it and Darth Vader's power, and Kenobi served no real dramatic purpose thereafter. The death of Luke's mentor was the solution to both problems. It fell to Bunny Aslup, the assistant to the producer, to type up the urgently rewritten scene, which she did using an old French manual typewriter, as her electric IBM model had broken on arrival in Tunisia.

In keeping with his idea of creating an entirely different kind of Hollywood film—one capable of surprising audiences in the way that foreign films had surprised him when he was a film student—Lucas thought about casting the Japanese actor Toshiro Mifune (*Rashomon* (1950), *Seven Samurai* (1954)) as Ben Kenobi. He reasoned that, if he went in this direction, the role of Princess Leia would go to a Japanese actor, too.

At the same time, however, Lucas also approached one of the most celebrated British actors of the 20th century, Alec Guinness, who was best known for his work with the director David Lean in the 1950s and '60s, including an Oscar-winning turn in *The Bridge on the River Kwai* (1957). ▸

▸ Guinness hesitated to accept the role of Obi-Wan Kenobi at first, believing that science-fiction films were not very interesting from an actor's point of view. He decided to give Lucas a chance, however, because he admired his work on *American Graffiti*, and because he was very impressed with the script. Guinness was eventually contracted in January 1976, just before Lucas settled on Harrison Ford, Mark Hamill, and Carrie Fisher as Han, Luke, and Leia.

Guinness and his wife arrived in Tunisia on March 24, 1976, and four days later the actor put on Obi-Wan Kenobi's outfit for the first time. A few days later, Lucas told Guinness that he had decided to kill Kenobi, but the character would live on, having become one with the Force—an idea Lucas had developed in his earlier scripts.

Guinness was not at all happy about being killed off, and even thought about quitting the film. But when cast and crew returned to England in April to shoot the interior scenes at Elstree Studios, Lucas took the veteran actor to lunch and explained how Obi-Wan's death not only made the story better, it made the character better: Now the old Jedi Master could really make an impact on the audience. Guinness agreed, and Kenobi's death scene was recorded at the end of May.

2 /

3 /

1 / (See previous page.) and 2 / Mark Hamill and Alec Guinness on set in Tunisia. Hamill recalled later that Guinness had a whimsical sense of humor and would make the younger actor explain details of the story that he didn't really need explaining, just to test him.

3 / The duel between Darth Vader and Obi-Wan Kenobi was shot over three days in May 1976. The actors used wooden blades that broke every time they touched them together, causing delays to the scene's completion.

4 / An early prototype of the lightsaber prop used by Alec Guinness as Obi-Wan Kenobi. (See opposite page.)

5 / Production designer John Barry used a First World War rod grenade to create the finished handle for Obi-Wan Kenobi's lightsaber. (See opposite page.)

4 /

Kenobi's death by lightsaber—and his own prowess with a blade—greatly heightened the impact of the weapons Lucas had first conceived as "lazer swords" in 1973. Inspired by Samurai blades and the swashbuckling films of Errol Flynn, Lucas described his idea for a "Jedi weapon" to concept artist Ralph McQuarrie, who depicted lightsabers for the first time. It then fell to special effects supervisor John Stears and his team to bring them to life on screen. They did this by designing a rotating wooden sword, partly coated with reflective material. Filming through a half-silvered mirror made the sword look as if it was illuminated from within. The color and outer glow were added later in post-production, using an animation technique called rotoscoping.

To complete the effect of the lightsaber, sound designer Ben Burtt created the distinctive buzz that would come to be imitated by children around the world. Actually the very first effect that Burtt created for the film, the now-familiar noise combined the humming of a film projector with the electronic crackle of a broken wire from an old television set.

5 /

OBI-WAN KENOBI DATA FILE

FIRST DAY OF SHOOTING: March 28, 1976

LAST DAY OF SHOOTING: June 16, 1976

FIRST LINE: "Hello there! Come here, my little friend. Don't be afraid." (To R2-D2, after the Tusken Raiders attack.)

LAST LINE: "Remember, the Force will be with you... always." (Luke hears Obi-Wan's Force spirit.)

6 /

7 /

8 /

6 / Keen diarist Alec Guinness observes proceedings on set. (See opposite page.)

7 / Mark Hamill and Alec Guinness posing with R2-D2 and C-3PO near the entrance to the Tatooine cantina. (See opposite page.)

8 / Alec Guinness on the Death Star set. Stunt supervisor Peter Diamond invented a new fighting style for the lightsaber duel between Obi-Wan and Darth Vader, as George Lucas didn't want anything that had been seen on screen before.

LEIA ORGANA

Princess Leia Organa of Alderaan is the youngest ever member of the Galactic Senate. Yet despite her youth, she represents her home planet with intelligence and diplomacy. She is secretly also a strong leader and a brilliant military strategist in the Rebel Alliance—just like her adoptive father, Viceroy Bail Organa, before her. Dedicated to the rebel cause, Leia does not hesitate to use her consular ship, the *Tantive IV*, or her status as a senator as cover for dangerous missions. Brave, resolute, and an expert shot with a blaster, she is surprisingly resistant to mind probes and intimidation, and could never betray the Rebellion—something neither Darth Vader nor Governor Tarkin expect when they capture the young princess.

There was a princess in *Star Wars* from the very beginning. Back in 1973, when George Lucas was working on his first ideas for the saga, under the title *Journal of the Whills, [Part] I*, he drew inspiration from Akira Kurosawa's 1958 masterpiece, *The Hidden Fortress*. Its story concerns two peasants who are mistaken for soldiers in a war and travel with a general and a princess who are trying to hide a treasure from their enemies. At first, the princess in Lucas' story was similarly a fairytale figure in the protection of an old soldier, but over a number of drafts, Lucas adapted the character of Leia into a strong, independent leader.

Choosing the right actress for the part of Leia was never going to be easy. Carrie Fisher auditioned for the role in London in December 1975, on the same day that Mark Hamill tried out for the part of Luke. The 19-year-old daughter of Hollywood stars Eddie Fisher and Debbie Reynolds, Fisher was just one of many young women to be considered on the day. The casting director, Dianne Crittenden, asked her to perform one scene in two different ways (a scene in which Leia revealed the importance of the data she had entrusted to R2-D2) and taped it. Fisher later said that she was sure she hadn't won the part, because she didn't hear back from anyone until three weeks afterward.

In fact, Lucas did have one other candidate in mind for the part, the singer and actor Terri Nunn (later the lead singer in the band Berlin). But he eventually conceded that Fisher was the right choice to portray a hard, strong leader who also had a warm heart.

Leia's clothers were designed by costume designer John Mollo and his team. Mollo used paper dolls to show his ideas to Lucas and checked with the production designer, John Barry, to be sure the costumes fit with the sets. Based on their feedback, he added a slit in Leia's dress, making it easier for her to move in action scenes, and had a pair of practical yet stylish boots specially made.

Fisher tried on the costume for the first time on April 20, 1976, together with the iconic sidebuns hairstyle that had been designed for her by makeup artist Patricia McDermott. This was the first hairstyle that Lucas approved of, having previously rejected at least 30 other designs! ▸

2 /

1 / Carrie Fisher as Leia. (See previous page.)

2 / Mark Hamill and Carrie Fisher on set in April 1976.

3 / The "Lash La Rue" scene as pictured by Ralph McQuarrie in November 1975. (See opposite page.)

4 / Matte painter Harrison Ellenshaw at work. His father, Peter, was a matte artist too, and won an Oscar for his work on *Mary Poppins* (1964). (See opposite page.)

5 / Despite her concerns, Fisher later confessed that she had enjoyed filming the rope-swing scene. (See opposite page.)

Long before Fisher was cast as Leia, in August 1975, Lucas met with John Barry and concept artist Ralph McQuarrie to discuss the sets that would be built for the film. Barry had an idea for a set that required Luke and Leia to swing across a chasm, located on the planet Alderaan. Though all scenes on Alderaan were later cut from the script, the concept endured, and was relocated to the Death Star, becoming one of the film's most famous scenes.

Lucas and co. referred to the sequence as the "Lash La Rue" scene, after the lasso-wielding cowboy film star of the 1940s and '50s (who would go on to work with Lucas a couple of years later, teaching Harrison Ford how to use a bullwhip for *Raiders of the Lost Ark*). The scene would require Luke to swing a grappling rope across a dizzying drop, an image that McQuarrie visualized in November 1975.

The scene was shot in April 1976. The crew tested the strength of the rope using lifesize dummies and layered the ground beneath with impact-absorbing cardboard boxes. Fisher was concerned that she might fall, drop her blaster, or lose her hairstyle during the take, but none of this happened and the scene was only filmed once. The drop on the set was about 12 feet, but a matte painting by Harrison Ellenshaw was added to the shot to give the illusion of a seemingly bottomless pit.

Hired in the later stages of the production, Ellenshaw came from Disney Studios to work on matte paintings for *Star Wars* between February and March 1977. Prior to this, McQuarrie had supplied many of the mattes that depicted planets in the background of the outer space shots. An established special effects technique since the early 20th century, matte images are made on glass, then overlaid on live-action footage. For *Star Wars*, this was done using an old Bell & Howell camera box.

3 /

4 /

5 /

PRINCESS LEIA DATA FILE

DAYS OF SHOOTING: 37

LAST DAY OF SHOOTING:
July 16, 1976

FIRST LINE:
"Darth Vader, only you could be so bold. The Imperial Senate will not sit still for this. When they hear you've attacked a diplomatic—" (To Vader as he boards Leia's diplomatic ship, the *Tantive IV*.)

LAST LINE:
"I knew there was more to you than money." (To Han Solo after he helps to destroy the Death Star.)

TRIVIA:
Leia was the last lead character to be cast.

6 /

7 /

8 /

9 /

6 / Leia originally shared a last name with her home planet, Organa Major. When the planet became Alderaan she kept the name Organa—though the name is never spoken by anyone in the film. (See opposite page.)

7 / For the closing celebration scene, shot in May 1976, George Lucas and Patricia McDermott designed a new hairstyle for Carrie Fisher called "hot plate special." (See opposite page.)

8 / In April 1976, Carrie Fisher shot her first important scene with Peter Cushing as Governor Tarkin. She had to look angry at him, but found it hard because Cushing was so sweet. She ended up picturing someone else to generate the right emotion.

9 / Behind-the-scenes with Harrison Ford, Mark Hamill, and Carrie Fisher. Fisher used to wear her famous "hairy earphones" (as she called them), and her costume all the time, even if she went out to buy something. The hairstyle was inspired by photos of Native Americans and Pancho Villa's rebel women by Edward S. Curtis.

HAN SOLO

The notorious spaceport of Mos Eisley may be one of the most dangerous places to visit on the planet Tatooine, but it is also where the best freighter pilots can be found. Some of them are just ordinary civilians, some work for the Empire, and others work for the Hutts, or one of the galaxy's other criminal syndicates. Ace pilot Han Solo has a bounty on his head because he jettisoned a shipment owned by Jabba the Hutt—head of the biggest crime family on Tatooine—when his ship was boarded by an Imperial cruiser. To save his life from bounty hunters, Solo must repay his debt to Jabba, and fast. So there are only two things that the captain of the *Millennium Falcon* and his Wookiee co-pilot, Chewbacca, need to worry about: money, and not running into any bounty hunters...

Ever since he appeared in George Lucas' very first concept for *Star Wars*—"*Journal of the Whills*"—Han Solo never changed his name, or his role as a friend and ally of the protagonist with a cowboy attitude. But it's not until the second draft, entitled "*Adventures of the Starkiller, Episode I: The Star Wars*" and completed in 1975, that he is given human form. Before then, the Ureallian alien Han Solo was "a huge green-skinned monster with no nose and large gills."

In Lucas' second draft, Han becomes humanoid—a young Corellian pirate who meets Luke Starkiller in a cantina and agrees to take him and his two droids to Organa Major, Princess Leia's home planet. Han is in debt to someone called Oxus, and doesn't have a ship of his own, so has to steal one. By Lucas' third draft, Solo has become the captain of a ship he had built himself, using money he borrowed from Jabba the Hutt. Now the Corellian finds himself badly indebted to Jabba.

While Lucas was writing the fourth draft—which made only minor changes to the Han Solo character—he started work on the casting, too. He went to New York, where one of the actors he interviewed for the part of Solo was Christopher Walken (along with Jodie Foster as a possible Princess Leia). Walken remained in the running for the part until the end, along with the African-American actor Glynn Turman, and Harrison Ford.

During a three-day casting session in December 1975, Lucas asked Ford to read Solo's lines each day, while other actors tried out for the roles of Luke and Leia. It was hardly surprising that Ford was perfect for the part, given that Lucas had had him in mind when he was writing it. But the director didn't want to cast any actor who had appeared in his previous film, *American Graffiti*, in which Ford played the role of out-of-town braggart Bob Falfa. In the end, the quality of Ford's test, and the dynamic between him and Mark Hamill as Luke, persuaded Lucas to cast him after all.

When he tried on Han Solo's costume, Ford didn't care for the shawl collar of his shirt, saying it was wrong for the character. He made the costume department take it off, and Lucas approved of his decision. This was not the only change Ford introduced to *Star Wars*, either. As Hamill and Carrie Fisher later recalled, his script had many notes written in the margins where he had made slight modifications to his lines. Ford's alterations didn't change what Solo was actually saying, just the way in which he said it, to more closely match his own conception of the character.

The result, skillfully judged in conjunction with his fellow actors' performances and Lucas' direction, is a character unlike any other in *Star Wars*, and one of cinema's most lovable rogues.

2 /

3 /

1 / Actor Harrison Ford on set near the *Millennium Falcon*. In 1970, Ford was cast in a small role in the film *Zabriskie Point*, but was cut from the final edit. He then left acting for a while and became a carpenter. Ford first met George Lucas when casting director Fred Roos, who was championing the young actor, hired him to fit a door at American Zoetrope—the independent film company founded by Lucas and Francis Ford Coppola in 1969. (See previous page.)

2 / Ford puts his arm around Chewbacca actor Peter Mayhew on set. Mayhew went on to play Chewie in *The Empire Strikes Back, Return of the Jedi, Revenge of the Sith* and *The Force Awakens*

.

3 / Ford playing Han Solo on the *Millennium Falcon* cockpit set.

4 / Han Solo's blaster was built by production designer John Barry, based on a German Mauser C96 pistol. (See opposite page.)

HAN SOLO DATA FILE

DAYS OF SHOOTING: 42

LAST DAY OF SHOOTING: June 24, 1976

In one of the first ideas Lucas had for the character's background, Han Solo had been raised by gypsies after he lost his parents in a space battle. Later, when he was seven years old, he lived with the Wookiees for about five years, before joining the Space Academy.

FIRST LINE
"Han Solo. I'm captain of the *Millennium Falcon*. Chewie here tells me you're looking for passage to the Alderaan system." Solo introducing himself to Luke Skywalker and Ben Kenobi.

LAST LINE
"Well, I wasn't gonna let you get all the credit and take all the reward." Han replies to Luke, who's very happy he came back and helped him destroy the Death Star.

5 /

5 / Mark Hamill and Harrison Ford take a break from a busy day's shooting.

CHEWBACCA

First mate on the *Millennium Falcon*, and the best friend of its captain Han Solo, Chewbacca is a 200-year-old Wookiee whose imposing presence can make even the bravest human fearful. According to Solo, Chewie—like all Wookiees—doesn't like to lose, particularly when he plays the holographic chess game, dejarik (he tends to pull his opponents' arms off when it happens). An experienced mechanic and a skilled shooter with his laser bowcaster, he is also a capable pilot.

Wookiees were invented by George Lucas in 1973, when the species name was initially spelled "Wookee." Setting out the ideas that would become *Star Wars*, Lucas described the creatures as eight-foot-tall, furry beasts that lived on the jungle world of Yavin.

In the rough draft written by Lucas a year later, Chewbacca was introduced as "the largest of the Wookees," with Han Solo (who, at that time, resembled a swamp creature), the only one who could speak his language. The striking alien pair set out to take over an Imperial outpost together, along with Jedi General Skywalker. It was only with the second draft, written by Lucas in 1975, that Chewbacca assumed his familiar role as the human Han Solo's co-pilot.

Lucas forged this version of Chewbacca as a combination of the furry Yavin beasts he had already conceived, and his own pet dog, Indiana—an Alaskan malamute who was often Lucas' own "co-pilot" in the passenger seat of his car.

To create a initial look for Chewbacca, concept artist Ralph McQuarrie made several sketches based on Lucas' descriptions and a drawing of a lemur that Lucas gave to him. Thereafter, it was makeup artist Stuart Freeborn's job to bring Chewbacca to life. Freeborn worked for many weeks on concepts and masks, trying to combine the various different animal elements—part monkey, part dog, part cat—that he and Lucas felt were essential to the character. The biggest challenge of all was creating a mask that could look fearsome one minute and friendly the next.

To play this surprisingly complex character, Lucas cast the seven-foot-tall British actor Peter Mayhew, who had just won his first film role as a robot Minotaur in fantasy film *Sinbad and the Eye of the Tiger*. Mayhew was talent-spotted for the part by a film producer who read about him in a newspaper article about people with big feet. At the time, Mayhew was working as deputy head porter in a London hospital.

For the voice of Chewbacca, Lucas turned to sound designer Ben Burtt. He explained that the character didn't speak English or any other intelligible language, but needed to be able to express emotion. While collecting sounds for the film at large, Burtt spent a lot of time in zoos recording animal calls and growls—most notably those of large mammals including bears, sea lions, and seals. Chewie's final, distinctive voice came about by combining several of these recordings, with particular prominence given to a walrus named Petulia, a black bear called Tarik, and a young cinnamon bear known as Pooh.

1 /

CHEWBACCA DATA FILE

FIRST DAY OF SHOOTING:
April 9, 1976

LAST DAY OF SHOOTING:
June 28, 1976

The Chewbacca costume was made from knitted mohair (goat and rabbit hair) and yak hair.

The word "Wookiee" first appeared in Lucas' directorial debut *THX 1138* (1971), when one of the characters says, "I think I just ran over a Wookiee."

2 /

3 /

1 / Chewbacca aims his trusty bowcaster. The nickname Chewie was initially scripted as the name of the rebel pilot who was later renamed Wedge Antilles.

2 / Makeup artist Stuart Freeborn works on the prototype Chewbacca mask in his studio. He would go on to design Jedi Master Yoda in *The Empire Strikes Back*.

3 / Stuart Freeborn with Chewbacca actor Peter Mayhew on the set of *Star Wars*. The area around Mayhew's eyes was blacked out with makeup as part of his Wookiee costume.

THE *FALCON* AND THE FLEET

She may be battered and scarred, but thanks to modifications made by her captain, Han Solo, the *Millennium Falcon* is the fastest piece of junk in the galaxy. Not only can she make point five past lightspeed and navigate the Kessel Run in the fewest number of parsecs, she can also hide her crew beyond the reach of Imperial sensors inside specially constructed smuggling compartments. However, the *Falcon* has been tinkered with so many times, she requires constant maintenance and her hyperdrive system can malfunction, leaving the ship at the mercy of her pursuers.

2 /

MILLENNIUM FALCON DATA FILE

Before it became the *Millennium Falcon*, Han Solo's ship was referred to by Lucas and the production team simply as "the pirate ship."

The full-size *Falcon* set was made of wood. It was built on Stage Three at Elstree and was so large that it couldn't be moved, with other sets having to be built around it.

Despite being spaced far apart in the film, nearly all the scenes that take place in the *Falcon*'s cockpit were filmed as one block on Stage Eight at Elstree.

The main hallway set was built on Stage Nine at Elstree.

The scene where Obi-Wan Kenobi senses the destruction of the planet Alderaan while on board the *Falcon* was filmed on Sir Alec Guinness' last day on set, June 16, 1976.

Han Solo's souped-up smuggling vessel was just a concept when George Lucas hired model maker Colin J. Cantwell to work alongside concept artist Ralph McQuarrie. Like several other members of the *Star Wars* crew, Cantwell had worked on Stanley Kubrick's legendary film, *2001: A Space Odyssey* (1968), a film that had deeply influenced Lucas. Yet the director steered Cantwell in a different direction from Kubrick's "hard" science-fiction, toward something closer to the comic-book aesthetic he grew up with. Cantwell became the "space consultant," drawing on his vast personal collection of spaceship models, to immediately start building prototypes for the various craft that would appear throughout the film.

Cantwell's models were vital to the production, as both the miniatures for the space battle scenes and the full-size cockpits and other ship interiors would be built to his designs. The process began with Cantwell developing a model, after which McQuarrie would visualize them in context in detailed paintings. The effects illustrator Joe Johnston and the art department would work up technical drawings and story-boards, and the special effects team would set about building the miniatures including all the external details specified in the previous stages. Finally came the creation of the full-size sets for shooting flesh-and-blood actors. Lucas would, of course, have to approve every one of these steps.

Cantwell spent several months perfecting his first concepts, with Han Solo's starship among them. Based on Cantwell's prototype of a long, linear vessel with lots of rocket boosters, McQuarrie came up with a painting and Johnston a design. The art team translated these into orthographic drawings, which, in turn, became an acrylic and plexiglas sculpture. All was well until a new science-fiction series debuted on British TV. The main spaceship in *Space: 1999* looked too much like Solo's, and so the decision was made to go back to the drawing board. Lucas decreed that the most important starship in the film needed to look more unconventional and unique, and in under a week, a new ship design was ready and approved.

Based on Lucas' descriptions, the new ship had a radial shape that looked heavily modified by its owner. The only element left from the earlier model was the cockpit, added onto the side to create an original, asymmetrical design. Lucas' handwritten notes for the fourth draft reflected the change, defining the new vessel a "pirate manta-ship." And the earlier design? Rather than being wastefully discarded—along with a large slice of the model budget—it was adapted to be Princess Leia's ship, the *Tantive IV*. ▸

1 / A Ralph McQuarrie painting showing the familiar shape of the Falcon—albeit without its final details—in one of the landing bays on board the Death Star. (See opposite page.)

2 / This Ralph McQuarrie concept piece from 1975 shows the initial version of Han Solo's ship on the planet Alderaan. At this stage, Alderaan was still the Imperial world where the princess was being held captive.

In 1976, production designer John Barry supervised the construction of the full-size *Millennium Falcon* exterior and interior, based on the second design and the blueprints created by the art department. It had to appear consistent with the miniature, but also be practical for filming, and so the main corridor and the communal area were built with removable panels that let in extra light. When all the scenes on board the *Falcon* had been shot, the corridor set was redressed and redecorated for use as the corridor of Leia's ship. But as the crew was preparing to shoot the opening scene—in which Darth Vader and his Imperial stormtroopers board the *Tantive IV* searching for the Death Star plans—Lucas realized that the set was not large enough for the battle sequence. Instead, Barry created a new set—a great white hallway that served as the perfect contrast to our first sight of Vader's entirely black armor.

3 /

4 /

5 /

3 / The miniature of the *Millennium Falcon* under construction by Industrial Light & Magic (ILM). The finished miniature was painted and intricately detailed to make it look realistically lived-in and battle-worn. It was then used to shoot the space battle sequences. (See opposite page.)

4 / The full-size *Falcon* set being constructed from blueprints drawn up by the art department, as seen on February 17, 1976. (See opposite page.)

5 / Mark Hamill (Luke), Alec Guinness (Obi-Wan), and Harrison Ford (Han) inside the full-size Falcon cockpit—a holdover from Colin J. Cantwell's original "pirate ship" design.

6 / Only half of the full-size *Falcon* build fit inside Stage Three at Elstree Studios. As the ship was too big to be moved, the sets for the Mos Eisley and Death Star landing bays were built around it.

6 /

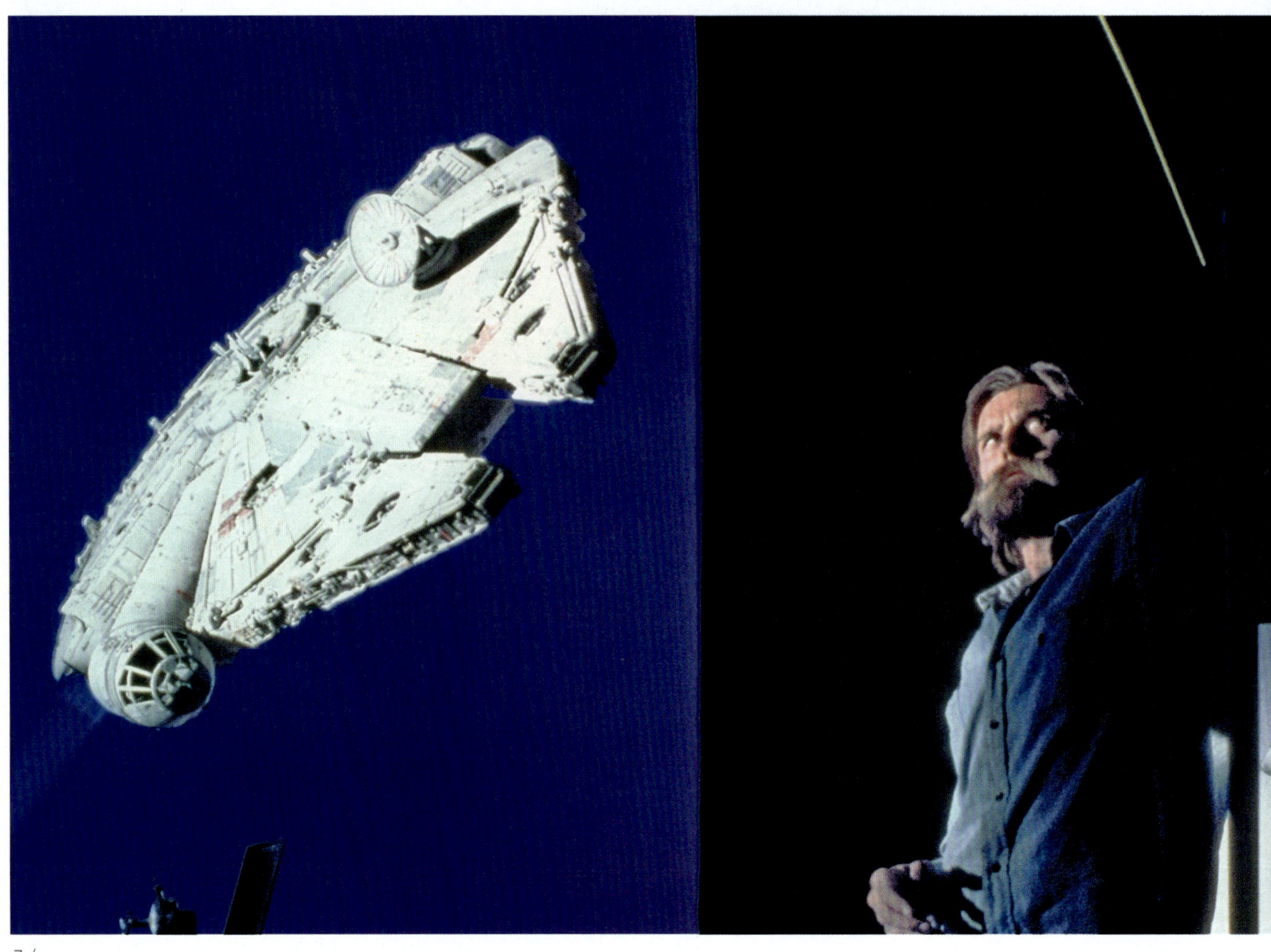

7 /

7 / The *Falcon* in front of bluescreen on ILM's shooting stage. A starfield background would be added later in postproduction.

8 / An X-wing fighter, shot with ILM's Dykstraflex motion-control camera system, built especially for *Star Wars*. (See opposite page.)

9 / Modelmaker David Jones in the ILM model shop with miniature X-wings, Y-wings, and a TIE fighter. (See opposite page.)

Of course, the *Millennium Falcon* was far from the only spacecraft in *Star Wars*, and in 1975, a year before filming began, Lucas made the decision to establish his own special effects company to better control all the outer space scenes. The company was Industrial Light & Magic (ILM), and it put Lucas in a position to do something that no other filmmaker had achieved before: create kinetic outer space action using miniatures that gave the illusion of being a real, live-action adventure.

One of Lucas' first ports of call when assembling the ILM team was the special effects artist John Dykstra, who assisted the effects supervisor Douglas Trumbull on Stanley Kubrik's *2001: A Space Odyssey*. Lucas showed Dykstra footage he had edited together of real aerial battles to convey what he wanted: fluid camera movement around the spaceships, as if it, and the audience, were among them. The project would call for about 350 effects shots, and they would need to be completed in two years. Conventional filmmaking wisdom said it was impossible, but Dykstra had been working on an idea for a new type of camera for a while, and joining ILM would give him the chance to build it.

A few weeks later, in an empty warehouse in Van Nuys, north of Los Angeles (rented for $2,300 per month), ILM set up shop. With two optical printers, a rotoscope department, two shooting stages, a model shop, a machine shop, and a woodshop—plus a team of talented and ambitious designers, animators, model builders, and production managers—the new company was born.

Though science-fiction special effects were nothing new in 1975, what made ILM different was its commitment to believability. In the past, filming a fleet of ships flying through space meant shooting all the elements separately (miniature ships, lasers, planets, the starfield background) and then combining them with an optical printer. Since it was nearly impossible to make identical camera movements for each element, such effects were nearly always shot from a static point of view, and would end up looking blatantly fake and two-dimensional. With *Star Wars* and ILM, Lucas planned to change all that—showing X-wings and TIE fighters that dived, weaved, and banked like real planes, so that the effects scenes appeared just as real as the ones with full-size sets, locations, and actors. ▶

8 /

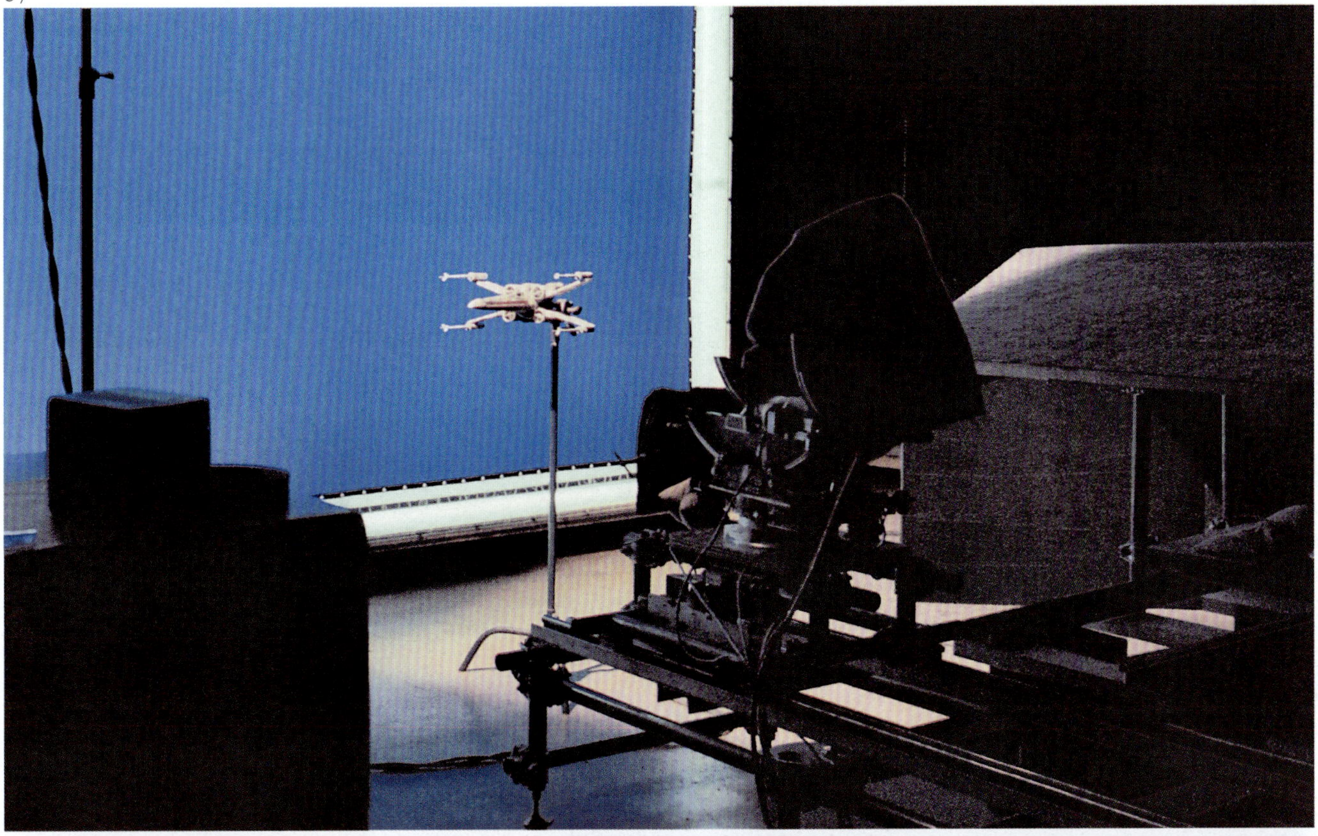

9 /

10 /

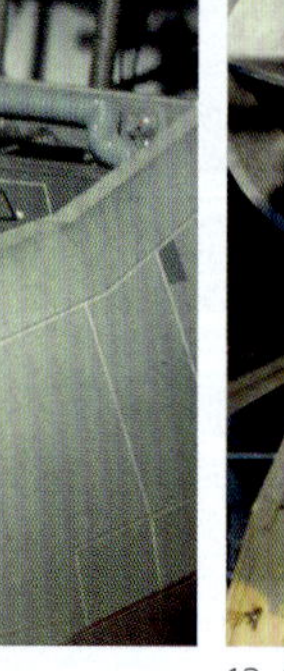

11 /

12 /

10 / Concept artwork by Ralph McQuarrie shows Y-wings in the rebel base on Yavin 4. Based on Colin J. Cantwell's models, the Y-wing design was finalized by Joe Johnston and was meant to suggest an old fighter that had been stripped down to make it airworthy once again.

11 / 12 / Inside the X-wing cockpit.

13 / The Yavin 4 hangar set, based on the concept art by Ralph McQuarrie. (See opposite page.)

14 / A miniature X-wing, complete with battle damage. The X-wing starfighters went through about seven iterations to reach this design. George Lucas saw the ships as similar to a dragster, with "a long narrow front and a guy sitting on the back." He added that, when the ship was ready to fight, it should draw its guns like a cowboy in a Western—the origin of the two wing positions, in Colin Cantwell's recollection. (See opposite page.)

Most of all, along with moving ships, Lucas wanted the camera to zoom, pan, or tilt as well, so that audiences would have the impression of being in the heart of the action—just like viewers of the aerial footage that Lucas had edited together and shown to Dykstra. Happily, the new kind of camera that the special effects man had in mind would be able to do just that.

Dykstra's idea was a motion-control camera system that could be programmed to photograph all the elements of a shot in exactly the same way over and over again. The camera, which the ILM team called the "Dykstraflex," was an amalgamation of three machines: a specialized camera, a mechanical rig, and an electronic controller. It was developed and perfected in the warehouse in Van Nuys over the course of about six months.

The many different miniature ships that would be shot by the Dykstraflex were developed using the same process that led to the *Millennium Falcon*. The X-wings, Y-wings, and TIE fighters were designed by Cantwell, Johnston, and McQuarrie based on Lucas' descriptions. After that, the ILM team would build the miniatures at their base in California, while production designer John Barry would supervise the construction of the full-size sets at Elstree in England. For the X-wings and Y-wings, Barry had models to refer to, but for everything else he had to wait until reference photographs could be shipped over from the U.S. When he saw that the ILM miniature-makers had used ready-made model kit parts to add realistic detail to their ships, Barry went out and bought large quantities of plumbing spares to recreate the look on a one-to-one scale. Many of these items then found use as a range of handheld props, including ray guns, lightsabers and Luke's comlink—which was actually part of a faucet!

13 /

14 /

15 /

15 / ILM art director Joe Johnston brought a rugged, mechanical reality to the often romanticized designs of Colin Cantwell and Ralph McQuarrie.

16 / Joe Johnston working on an early model of Han Solo's ship, before it was repurposed as the *Tantive IV* (note the radar dish and the esape pods).

17 / Grant McCune and Doug Smith of ILM get the Imperial Star Destroyer ready for the unforgettable first shot of the film. A very close camera pass across the 3 ft model made it look huge on screen. (See opposite page.)

18 / Only one full-size X-wing and one full-size Y-wing were built. The rest of the Yavin 4 hangar set was filled with two-dimensional painted cut-outs of the ships. (See next spread.)

16 /

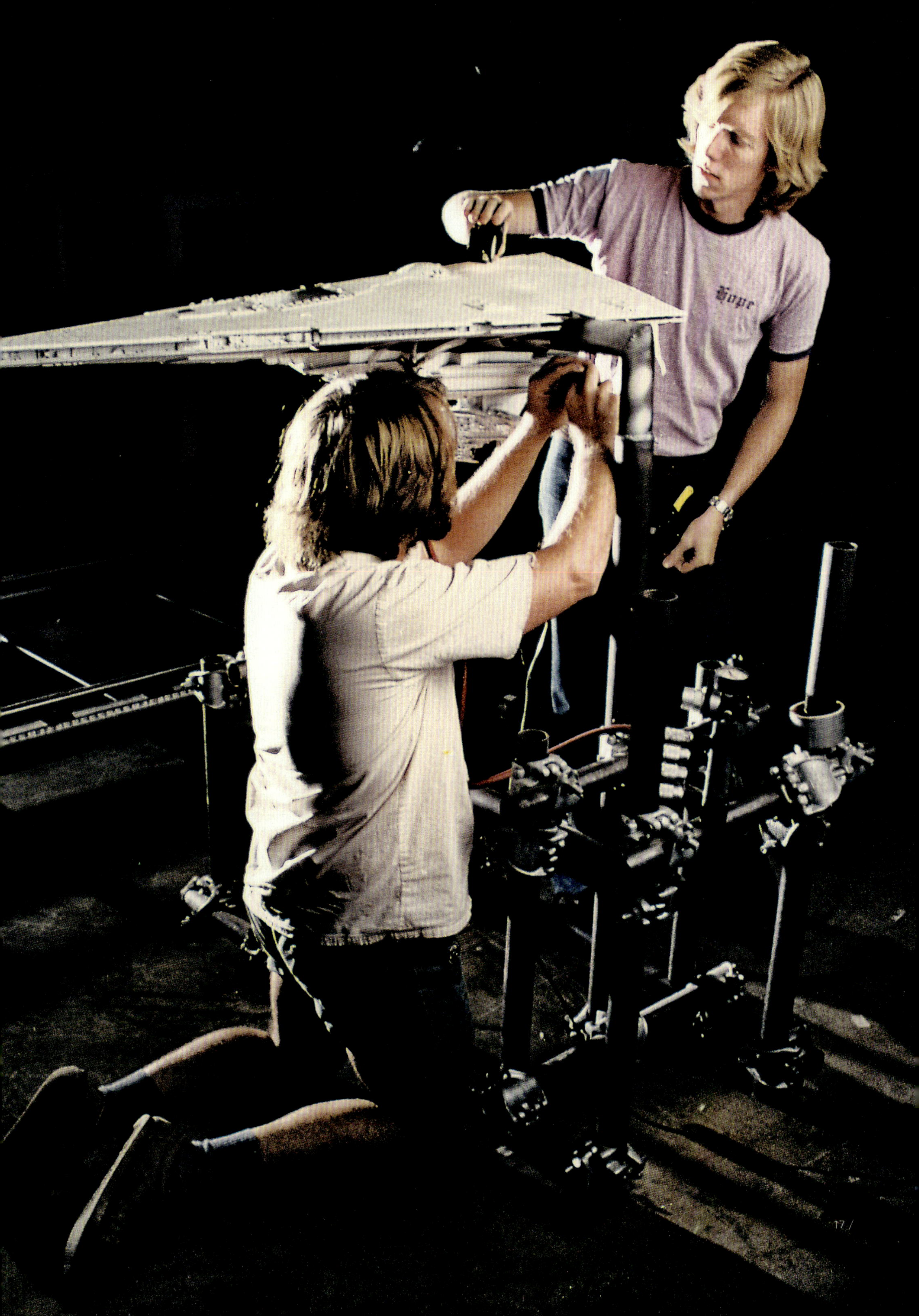

66

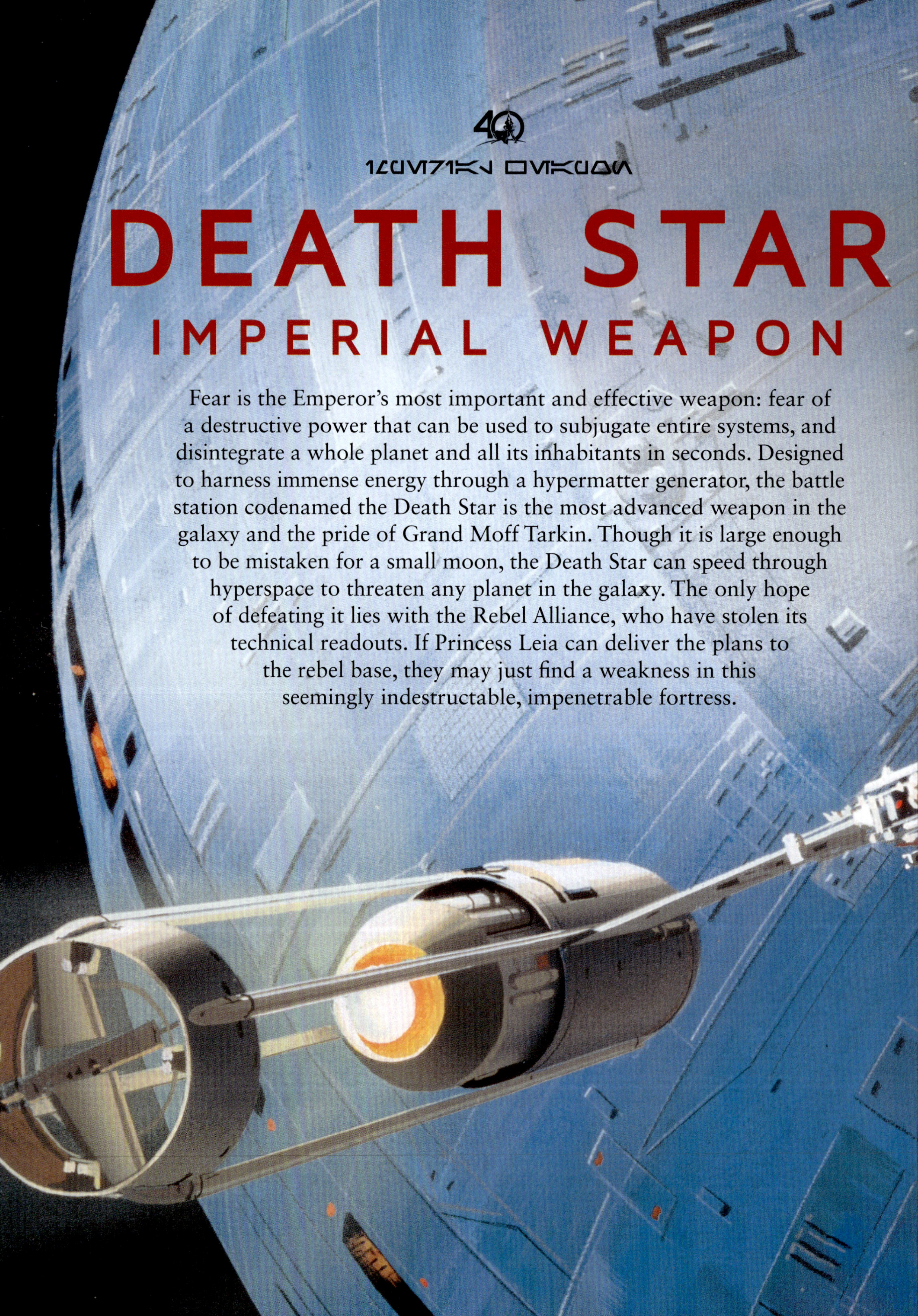

DEATH STAR

IMPERIAL WEAPON

Fear is the Emperor's most important and effective weapon: fear of a destructive power that can be used to subjugate entire systems, and disintegrate a whole planet and all its inhabitants in seconds. Designed to harness immense energy through a hypermatter generator, the battle station codenamed the Death Star is the most advanced weapon in the galaxy and the pride of Grand Moff Tarkin. Though it is large enough to be mistaken for a small moon, the Death Star can speed through hyperspace to threaten any planet in the galaxy. The only hope of defeating it lies with the Rebel Alliance, who have stolen its technical readouts. If Princess Leia can deliver the plans to the rebel base, they may just find a weakness in this seemingly indestructable, impenetrable fortress.

2 /

1 / One of the first Death Star illustrations by concept artist Ralph McQuarrie, finished in February 1975. In this concept for the space station, a laser cannon charged inside the core would emerge from the opening at the pole. (See previous spread.)

2 / Grand Moff Tarkin (Peter Cushing) in the Death Star conference room. This set posed many challenges for director of photography Gil Taylor. First of all, the dark blue walls had to be repainted about seven shades lighter in order to be properly lit, and even then the number of floodlights needed distorted some of the equipment.

3 / The trench run, as depicted by Ralph McQuarrie. In this early version of the scene, the walls of the Death Star trenches are flatter and its cannons lower than in the miniatures later built by ILM. (See opposite page.)

4 / A Death Star model hand-painted by Ralph McQuarrie, ready to be shot on bluescreen by the Dykstraflex motion-control camera. (See opposite page.)

Ever since the first draft of what would become *Star Wars*, written in 1974, George Lucas imagined Imperial forces striking Leia's home planet—then called Aquilae—using a space fortress called the Death Star. But it was only in the second draft, 1975's *Adventures of the Starkiller, Episode I: The Star Wars*, that the fortress evolved from being just a wandering space station, carrying troops and spaceships, to become a superweapon and a determining factor in the story.

Now, in a way, the Death Star was a character in itself, with the power to wipe out the protagonists and their friends. To destroy this new enemy, the hero, Luke, needed help from the Aquillian ranger Bail Antilles, and droids R2-D2 (who helped get Luke's ship into position) and C-3PO (who fired the blast that destroyed the Death Star).

While working on the third draft, Lucas moved this focus to a duel between Luke and Darth Vader on board the battle station, overshadowing the rebel attack and the destruction of the Death Star. But by the fourth draft the duel was gone, and the breakneck space race to the weakness in the Death Star was restored. In this version, Luke fired the shot that destroyed the battle station.

The design of the Death Star was based on paintings by Ralph McQuarrie and a concept model by Colin Cantwell. It was always envisioned as a sphere, but was subject to some design revisions, including a major increase in size.

When the Industrial Light & Magic (ILM) team started work on the Death Star miniature in 1975, they immediately realized that one battle station was not enough. They needed different models at different scales. For the dogfight with the Death Star in the background, a small-scale prop of the whole station was called for, as a background matte painting would not allow for the changes in perspective that the frenetic space battle required.

Next, for closer shots of the station exterior, ILM built two different large-scale models of the detailed surface, that were used to create the impression of ships flying over it at differing heights. These models had to be built flat so that cameras could run along them on rails, but the ILM team calculated that some curvature should still be visible, given the scale specified for the station in the script. To overcome this problem, it was agreed that the fictional size of the station would be radically increased.

Finally, for the "trench run" sequence that sees ships descend right into the architecture of the Death Star, a further model was needed with even more levels of detail. To achieve this, the ILM team built eight highly detailed miniatures and arranged them in different combinations to create the illusion of a 60-foot trench, ending with the exhaust port. Each trench section measured two feet deep by three feet wide, and all were given extra detail in the form of thousands of pieces of retro-reflective tape, representing windows.

3 /

4 /

DEATH STAR DATA FILE

Sound designer Ben Burtt used the same thunderclap sound (a combination of thunder and a struck sheet of metal) for explosions during the end battle on the Death Star, and the exploding main hatch on Leia's ship at the start of the film.

The Death Star detention level set was built on Stage Four at Elstree Studios in the U.K. Its floor was made of plastic fork-lift truck pallets.

Industrial Light & Magic worked on the *Millennium Falcon*'s escape from the Death Star from September 1976 to January 1977.

ILM completed the final battle sequence in April 1977—just one month before the film came out in theaters!

5 /

6 /

5 / Special effects cinematographer Richard Edlund shoots an explosion on the second of the two Death Star surface miniatures in the ILM parking lot.

6 / The larger scale Death Star trench miniature in the ILM parking lot.

7 / An explosion on one of the two mid-scale Death Star surface miniatures in the ILM parking lot. (See opposite page.)

8 / The ILM team gathered together in front of the Death Star surface miniature on February 4, 1977. (See opposite page.)

7 /

8 /

9 /

10 /

11 /

12 /

13 /

9 / Han Solo and Chewbacca fight for their lives inside the Death Star. The blast doors are shaped to suggest that they close diagonally. In fact, they slide in and out horizontally. (See opposite page.)

10 / On the Death Star control room set with Peter Cushing as Grand Moff Tarkin. (See opposite page.)

11 / Ralph McQuarrie's key illustration showing the dogfight within the Death Star trenches. Finished in November 1975, it shows the final designs for the X-wing starfighter and the TIE fighter, as approved by George Lucas.

12 / 13 / Production illustrations by Ralph McQuarrie were used by George Lucas and the second production unit as a guide for the sequence in which the *Millennium Falcon* is caught in a tractor beam and pulled into the Death Star. The background seen in the film is actually a matte painting, while the stormtroopers seen in the foreground are both played by Joe Johnston, shot using split-screen.

STORMTROOPERS

SOLDIERS OF THE EMPIRE

Born out of the clone army that once defended the Galactic Republic, Imperial stormtroopers are now the most visible symbol of the Empire's rule across the galaxy. Highly disciplined and loyal to the Emperor, each trooper is conditioned to follow orders without question. The distinctive white stormtrooper armor enables its wearer to survive in many different environments and is equipped with power packs, energy rations, and tools such as grappling hooks, comlinks, and macrobinoculars. Often deployed in vast numbers, stormtroopers are trained never to be distracted by casualties in their own ranks, and overwhelm their enemies as a faceless tide. Their anonymity can also be a weakness, should an opponent be brave enough to don stormtrooper armor and infiltrate their ranks.

The shock troops of the Empire were present in George Lucas' story ideas for *Star Wars* from the very first draft. Their iconic white armor was designed by artist Ralph McQuarrie, based on Lucas' detailed early descriptions. Once approved, it then fell to costume designer John Mollo and his assistants to bring the concept art to life as a functional outfit suitable for highly mobile performers.

The completed costume was made up of: a black all-in-one bodysuit, front and back torso panels, shoulder pieces, upper and lower arm pieces connected by black elastic, leg panels that attached to a belt, rubber gloves, and elasticated boots that were painted white. On March 18, 1976—just four days before the shoot in the Tunisian desert was due to begin—Lucas told Mollo he needed some stormtroopers on location, and that they had to be in "combat order." With little time to spare, Mollo and his team visited a Boy Scout shop in London, bought some backpack racks, and augmented them with plastic seed boxes, some plastic drainpiping, and some lab pipe, before painting each assembly black. To indicate rank, Mollo painted biker's chest protectors black and orange and added them to the shoulders of the costumes. The "combat order" troopers were ready to shoot!

1 /

2 /

1 / Ralph McQuarrie's concept art for the stormtroopers from March 1975, showing the iconic armor for the first time. At this time, stormtroopers used lightsabers and carried shields. Han Solo (on the left), is also equipped with a lightsaber, and is flanked by Luke and Chewbacca (carrying Luke's brother, Deak).

2 / Photographed on the fourth day of filming in Tunisia, six local men were hired to play the "combat order" stormtroopers.

STORMTROOPER DATA FILE

Lucas wanted the troopers to be white for two reasons. Firstly, because white, gray, and black are the colors of the technological world, as opposed to the colors of the natural world, namely tan, brown, and green. Secondly, because he didn't want all the bad guys to be dressed in dark colors.

Lucas and sound designer Ben Burtt added voices for some of the stormtroopers when they worked on the fourth final audio mix in May 1977 (when the film had already been released in theaters).

Mark Hamill and Harrison Ford couldn't sit down in their stormtrooper outfits, so were given sawhorses to perch on.

Stunt supervisor Peter Diamond and his stunt performer colleagues Reg Harding and Colin Skeaping played various different stormtroopers and performed most of the trooper falls.

After principal photography wrapped in July 1976, most of the stormtrooper armor was stolen, leaving the crew with just one full costume for the last few takes.

3 /

4 /

5 /

6 /

7 /

3 / The "combat order" stormtroopers created by costume designer John Mollo, seen on March 25, 1976—the first day of shooting in Tunisia. (See opposite page.)

4 / Chewbacca with Han and Luke in their stolen stormtrooper gear on board the Death Star. (See opposite page.)

5 / Stormtroopers blast their way into detention block AA-23 during the rescue of Princess Leia. (See opposite page.)

6 / Desert-distressed costume detailing on a stormtrooper helmet in Tunisia in March '76.

7 / A stormtrooper crosses the Tatooine desert on the back of a local sand creature, the dewback.

TATOONE

THE DESERT WORLD

The Outer Rim Territories are the largest region in the known galaxy and the farthest from the Core Worlds. Tatooine is one of the frontier planets in the Outer Rim, orbiting two suns, Tatoo I and Tatoo II. It has a hot, dry atmosphere, and its arid surface is covered in sand dunes and canyons. The absence of water makes many regions, such as the Jundland Wastes, almost uninhabitable. Where there is life, the planet's remoteness attracts outlaws and smugglers, who use spaceports such as Mos Eisley to conduct their business—often involving crime boss Jabba the Hutt. The planet is also home to dangerous Tusken Raiders, the mysterious Jawas, and moisture farmers such as Owen Lars, who extract water from the atmosphere using vaporator towers. Tatooine doesn't offer much in the way of adventure for an homest young man, as Lars' nephew, Luke Skywalker, knows only too well.

1 /

TATOOINE DATA FILE

FIRST DAY OF SHOOTING:
March 22, 1976

LAST DAY OF SHOOTING:
April 4, 1976

Tunisian places used as locations included Nefta, Tozeur, Matmata, and Ajim (Djerba).

Most sets and equipment were sent from England to Europe and then onto Tunisia by road, but the final shipment had to be sent by aircraft just two days before shooting, at a cost of $20,000.

The name "Tatooine" comes from Tataouine, a city in south Tunisia.

1 / This concept painting by Ralph McQuarrie shows Luke on a cliff overlooking Mos Eisley. The character of Luke was concieved as a girl at the time it was painted in April 1975.

2 / Inspired by Ralph McQuarrie's art, this location photo shows R2-D2, C-3PO, Obi-Wan Kenobi, and Luke Skywalker on the cliff overlooking Mos Eisley. (See opposite page.)

One of the first things George Lucas did in 1973 as he began to write his outer space epic was to make a list of names. Desert planets called "Aquilae" and "Yoshiro" were on the list from the start. But the notion of a desert planet warmed by twin suns first appeared in 1974, as two robots, C-3PO and R2-D2, find themselves walking across the dune sea of "Utapau". The planet Utapau became Tatooine in the fourth draft of the script in 1976, but Lucas remembered the name and used it for another Outer Rim world, characterized by gigantic sinkholes, in *Revenge of the Sith* in 2005.

Of course, it's not insignificant that Tatooine has twin suns. Twins are part of Lucas' story from the very first draft, in which Luke has two twin brothers called Windy and Biggs. Twins are a key storytelling device in many different mythologies, where they are often credited with special powers.

In 1975, during a scouting trip to Tunisia to find the desert location that would serve as Tatooine, production supervisor Robert Watts and production designer John Barry visited the island of Djerba and the town of Matmata (where the inhabitants sometimes live underground to escape the heat). The Tunisian landscape and buildings inspired Lucas, who came up with ideas for Tatooine's architecture and the look of the Lars homestead.

For the desert shoot, Barry dressed Djerba as the spaceport of Mos Eisley, and 45 extras were hired to populate the set: four as Tusken Raiders, four as starpilots, four as stormtroopers, three as robots, 12 children as Jawas, and 16 men and women as farmers.

2 /

The first time that Lucas used the name "Tusken" was in the second draft of his story, where it referred to special agents working for the Empire. The Tusken Raiders seen in the film—primitive tribesmen native to Tatooine—appeared only in 1975 with the third draft. As Luke, C-3PO, and R2-D2 cross the desert in search of Ben Kenobi, they make camp and are attacked by Raiders, who strap Luke onto an electric windmill. When the special effects for the windmill were deemed far too expensive, however, Lucas decided to cut the entire scene.

Another species indigenous to Tatooine, the small, scavenging Jawas, were originally huge, grey beasts. They only became dwarf-like traders in the second draft. Inspired by the "shelldwellers" of his earlier film, *THX 1138*, Lucas imagined the Jawas as filthy little rats, but felt the initial prototype costume was too theatrical. He worked with costume designer John Mollo to perfect the design, with the addition of little brown cloaks with a Russian Cossack hoods and scarves. The faces of the Jawa performers were hidden behind black stocking masks, in front of which light-up eyes shone out unblinkingly.

The Jawas' desert transport, the mighty, caterpillar-tracked sandcrawler, was designed by model maker Colin Cantwell, then revised by concept artist Ralph McQuarrie. Production designer John Barry built the interior and partial exterior of the full-size sandcrawler, while Industrial Light & Magic (ILM) created a miniature for the long shots. The full set was used in Tunisia, while the model was shot in the desert of Randsburg, California, in early 1977.

3 /

4 /

5 /

6 /

3 / Tusken Raiders in the Tatooine desert with their distinctive Gaderffii stick weapons. (See opposite page.)

4 / Ralph McQuarrie's key illustration for the Tusken Raiders and their bantha mounts, from 1975. McQuarrie said that he imagined countless battles taking place above Tatooine, with wreckage falling from the sky to be buried in the sand.

5 / The Jawas in the Tunisian desert. Their leader was played by the British actor Jack Purvis, who was also the long-time cabaret partner of R2-D2 actor, Kenny Baker. The other Jawas were played by local children.

6 / The Jawas carry R2-D2 off to their sandcrawler. For the Jawas' voices, sound designer Ben Burtt altered the voices of crew members speaking and yelling words from African dialects that he had studied previously.

7 /

Throughout the creation of *Star Wars*, many characters changed their name, role, and look, while many events were transformed or excised altogether. The cantina scene, however, remained largely unchanged ever since its genesis in 1973. The scene, in which Luke Skywalker and Obi-Wan Kenobi meet Han Solo and Chewbacca, is crucial not only because it sees Obi-Wan use his lightsaber on screen for the first time, but also because it depicts an incredible array of alien creatures and exotic monsters, the likes of which had never been seen on screen before.

The talents of George Lucas, costume designer John Mollo, sound designer Ben Burtt, and makeup artist Stuart Freeborn (who worked with his wife, son, and six assistants) combined to give the 42 extras hired for the scene the greatest possible impact. Composer John Williams then wrote the music played by the cantina band based on Lucas' specific request: alien musicians playing a 1930s swing record!

8 /

7 / Aliens of all shapes and sizes populate the cantina set at Elstree Studios in England. (See previous spread.)

8 / Stunt supervisor Peter Diamond as one of the Tusken Raiders that attacks Luke (Mark Hamill). Diamond and Hamill rehearsed the scene out of costume, but once Diamond had his Tusken headgear on, he could no longer see what he was doing. For that reason, the fear in Hamill's eyes is real!

9 / "Wanted men" Dr. Evazan—who has the death sentence in 12 systems—and Ponda Baba, who has just lost his arm while trying to fire his blaster at Obi-Wan Kenobi. In this moment, the audience realizes that Kenobi remains a Jedi Master and a skilled warrior. (See opposite page.)

10 / The Mos Eisley extras in their alien costumes. Among them is the bounty hunter Greedo (back row, second from right), played by actor Paul Blake, a friend of C-3PO performer, Anthony Daniels. (See following spread.)

9 /

10 /

THE FOURTH MOON OF YAVIN

The galaxy is incredibly vast and full of worlds of all sizes—from small moons to gas giant planets. Not all of them host sentient life or are hospitable to humans, and some have never even been explored. If a world cannot be exploited, it is of little interest to the Empire and goes ignored by its forces. The remote fourth moon of the red gas giant Yavin is just such a world, and so the Rebel Alliance made it their secret base of operations, deep in the Outer Rim Territories. Hidden in thick jungle, inside an ancient Massassi temple, the base is equipped with a command center, briefing rooms, and a hangar big enough for X-wing and Y-wing fighter squadrons and the *Millennium Falcon*.

1 / One of the last key illustrations to be completed by Ralph McQuarrie, showing rebel ships leaving Yavin 4, with a rebel guard in the foreground. To shoot the scene inspired by this painting, cinematographer Richard Edlund, designer Richard Alexander, and second unit production manager Pepi Lenzi left for Guatemala in March 1977. They were accompanied by visual effect artist Lorne Peterson who plays the rebel guard, and a garbage can that served as the lookout tower! They found the perfect location atop Temple III in the ancient city of Tikal. (See previous spread.)

2 / Alex McCrindle (General Dodonna) and Carrie Fisher (Princess Leia) on the Yavin 4 command center set.

3 / Completed in December 1975, this Ralph McQuarrie painting shows the medal ceremony taking place in the Massassi throne room on Yavin 4.

2 /

3/

YAVIN 4 DATA FILE

The medal ceremony was shot from May 13 to May 18, 1976, on Stage H at Shepperton Studios.

In June, Stage H was turned into the rebel hangar before George Lucas decided it was too small.

Larry Cuba created the then-state-of-the-art computer graphics seen in the briefing room for $10,200.

George Lucas first conceived of a jungle world called Yavin in 1973. In his early notes for *Star Wars*, he imagines a planet with that name that is home to the hairy, eight-foot-tall Wookiees. In his second draft—completed in January 1975—he makes the lush location a moon in orbit around the main planet, and establishes it as the secret stronghold of the rebel forces.

Lucas envisioned the base as a ruined temple, with X-wing and Y-wing starfighters arrayed impressively on an airfield right outside. However, budgetary constraints and logistical issues saw the ships relocated to an indoor flight deck for the final film. In order to keep the scenes as technically straightforward as possible, Lucas lit the space with in-camera lamps designed to look like part of the hangar, and keep the rest of the location as dark as possible.

The hangar itself was built on a 250-foot sound stage at Shepperton Studios in England. Despite being a very impressive space, it was still too small to realize Lucas' vision without camera trickery. So, to make it appear even larger, production designer John Barry built the back half of the hangar as a perspective model, complete with flat, cutout ships. Regular repositioning of the hero X-wing props also added to the sense of a much larger fleet.

For the other major Yavin 4 set—the throne room where Leia awards Luke and Han's medals—scale was achieved a different way: by using almost 400 background performers! There was no budget to create that many outfits from scratch, so the costume department dressed the extras in stock items: US Marine and French Foreign Legion uniforms, augmented with various hats and scarves.

4 / 

5 / 

6 / 

4 / Ralph McQuarrie's key illustration for the temple exterior was completed in April 1975, and closely resembles the base seen in the finished film.

5 / Matte artist Harrison Ellenshaw works on the background painting used to represent the temple exterior in the film.

6 / Ralph McQuarrie depicted this early concept for the Y-wing fighter on an airfield outside the temple base, before an indoor location was settled on.

JOHN WILLIAMS COMPOSER

John Williams was born in Floral Park, New York, in 1932. He rose to prominence in the late 1950s working with the composer Henry Mancini on the music for TV shows such as *Peter Gunn* (1958-1961), before winning acclaim as a composer of big-screen scores. Academy Award nominations in 1967 and 1969 were followed by a win for his *Fiddler on the Roof* score in 1971. In 1974, Williams worked with director Steven Spielberg for the first time, forging a relationship that would see the pair collaborate on the likes of *Jaws* (1975), *E.T. The Extra-Terrestrial* (1982), and the *Indiana Jones* films (1981, 1984, 1989, 2008). In 1976, while working with Spielberg on *Close Encounters of the Third Kind* (1977), he met George Lucas for the first time.

When George Lucas approached John Williams to write the score for *Star Wars*, he explained that he didn't want any electronic music or outer space sounds. Everything else in the film was so new that the music had to be symphonic to give the audience something reassuringly familiar to relate to.

Williams began work on the score in January and February 1977, developing themes for the main scenes and characters. He chose not to draw on existing pieces of classical music, in the belief that the film called for its own themes, strongly related to the situations and the characters, something he later defined as "a solid dramaturgical glue."

Recording began on March 5, 1977, with Williams conducting the London Symphony Orchestra at the Anvil Studios in Denham, England. Released as an album in the summer, the soundtrack won the composer his third Oscar and became one of the biggest-selling movie scores of all time. In 2017, Williams recorded the music for his eighth *Star Wars* movie!

1 /

2 /

3 /

1 / John Williams conducts the London Symphony Orchestra. *Star Wars* marked the first time the composer used a full symphony orchestra for one of his movie soundtracks. (See opposite page.)

2 / John Williams (center) at work in the recording studio. Director Steven Spielberg strongly recommended the composer to George Lucas, who wanted a romantic and old-fashioned sound for *Star Wars*.

3 / Williams conducts the London Symphony Orchestra as the film is projected on a big screen in front of him. Luke's theme had to be noble, but also bold and brassy, and was mainly performed by the brass section.

WORLDWIDE SUCCESS

Released in more than 900 theaters in Canada and the United States by October 1977, *Star Wars* soon became Twentieth Century Fox's number one film of all time. Meanwhile, it was released in the most important foreign markets, dubbed into French, German, Italian, and Spanish, and subtitled in Chinese, Arabic, and Japanese. But it was just the beginning of a long story: *Star Wars* was re-released in 1978, 1979 (along with the first trailer for *The Empire Strikes Back*), 1981 (now with the title Episode IV: *A New Hope*), and 1982. The Special Edition hit theaters in 1997, when *A New Hope* returned to the number one spot at the U.S. box office for three more weeks.

1 /

2 /

1 / The original British "quad" poster from 1977, by the Brothers Hildebrandt. (See opposite page.)

2 / An original 1977 "A-style" poster known to collectors by the ID code 77/21-0.

3 / Clockwise from top left: Posters from Germany, France, Hong Kong, and Italy.

3 /